THIRD EDITION

W9-BBQ-661

COLLEGE & UNIVERSITY
BUDGETING

An Introduction for Faculty
and Academic Administrators

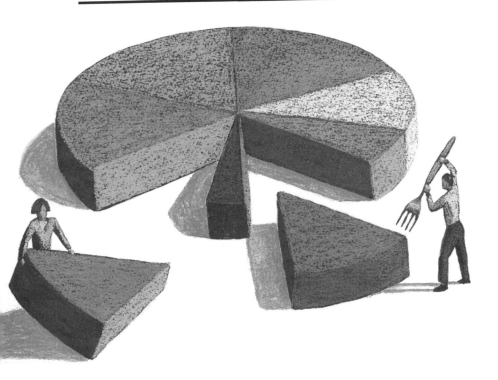

NACUBO

LARRY GOLDSTEIN

Library of Congress Cataloging-in-Publication Data

Goldstein, Larry, 1950–
   College & university budgeting : an introduction for faculty and academic administrators / by Larry Goldstein. -- 3rd ed.
     p. cm.
   Rev. ed. of: College and university budgeting / Richard J. Meisinger, Jr. 2nd ed. c1994.
   Includes bibliographical references and index.
   ISBN 1-56972-031-2
   1. Universities and colleges--United States--Finance. 2. Universities and colleges--United States--Business management. I. Title: College and university budgeting. II. Meisinger, Richard J., 1945– College and university budgeting. III. Title.

LB2342.M43 2005
378'.02'0973--dc22

2004064981

National Association of College and University Business Officers
Washington, DC
www.nacubo.org

Printed in the United States of America

CONTENTS

ACKNOWLEDGMENTS

My greatest thanks are extended to Richard J. Meisinger, Jr., author of the first and second editions of this book. Without his well-laid foundation, the task of writing this edition would have been immeasurably more difficult. I hope that he will look kindly on my extensive reliance on the same words he used to convey so many of the issues presented in the book.

I also would like to thank NACUBO's publications director, Donna Klinger, whose patience was tested beyond reason as I continually missed deadlines. She proved to be very understanding and, more important, encouraging and supportive throughout the process. Special recognition also is due Karen Colburn, who helped guide this first-time author through the process of moving a manuscript from rough draft to publication. My thanks also go to editor Ellen Hirzy, who applied her significant talents to make the book considerably more readable.

I wish to acknowledge my many current and former colleagues in higher education financial management—those on campuses as well as those working in the association community and the commercial sector serving higher education. It would be impossible to list every name, but many have contributed greatly to my education and professional development. Several individuals were particularly helpful to me as I worked on this project, including Melody Bianchetto, Tom Leback, and Colette Sheehy of the University of Virginia; James Elsass and Ingrid Stafford of Northwestern University; Terri Gehr of Columbus State Community College; and Cathy Statham of the National Center for Education Statistics.

Finally, I dedicate this book to my wife, Sue, and our children—Amy, Heather, and Peter. Each of them contributed to this book in various ways, most significantly by allowing me to take time away from them to devote to my career on campus and in the association community. I'm forever in their debt.

Larry Goldstein
Crimora, Virginia
December 2004

PREFACE

The budget is a critical tool for colleges and universities. In relatively lean times like those we have experienced in recent years, it takes on even greater significance. When resources are more plentiful, less attention is paid to the budget. Instead, faculty and staff go about their daily campus activities spending as needed with the confidence that financial problems will be addressed should they arise.

That is clearly not the case in the present environment. It is a given that not-for-profit organizations—both independent and governmental—never have sufficient resources to accomplish everything they would like to do. No matter how much they have, there always is more that could be done, or they could improve the quality of current activities and programs. As this third edition of *College and University Budgeting: An Introduction for Faculty and Academic Administrators* is being written, however, many organizations are facing the real question of whether existing service portfolios can be sustained. For some, the question is even more critical: Can the institution survive? Unlike past periods, when higher education institutions added programs and activities with relatively little regard for their impact on the overall budget, in the current climate even elite campuses are cutting faculty positions or eliminating entire programs.

Unfortunately, nothing in this volume will create additional resources for any campus. At best, one might hope that by understanding the higher education budgeting environment, organizations and those working in them will make wise spending decisions. Without an increased emphasis on obtaining maximum value for each invested dollar, more and more campuses will be forced to deal with program elimination and service reductions. Time used in this way, though essential under certain conditions, is not rewarding from a personal standpoint, and it is not what stimulates faculty and administrators to pursue careers in the academy. Any effort focused on cutting programs is a distraction from the primary objectives of improving academic quality and enhancing service delivery.

The intended audience for this primer includes new academic administrators and faculty members who seek involvement in campus governance and need a greater understanding of administrative processes, particularly those related to budgets and budgeting. This book also should be of value to academic and financial officers who are interested in enhancing the role of interested faculty in the budget process. And as more campuses look outside higher education when filling administrative vacancies, staff who are new to the field can use the book to move quickly along the learning curve.

After reading this book, readers will have a better understanding of the budget process at their institutions. They will be able to ask meaningful questions about the process and budget components, and they will be equipped to make valuable contributions. The culture of the institution will influence the likelihood of readers obtaining responses to the questions they raise. Similarly, the historical role of faculty will influence when and how they are invited to participate and determine how their input is used. For the most part, however, the more knowledgeable and informed they are, the more likely they are to offer constructive advice and receive answers to their important questions about the budget process.

Chapter 1 provides an introduction to budgets and the budgetary process, with a brief explanation of why budgeting is an important element of policy making. This chapter includes information about the critical linkage of budgets to planning. It explains what a budget is and how it goes beyond mere numbers in describing what an institution is all about. The chapter clarifies why the budgeting process is important and why it receives so much attention, especially when there are few resources to allocate. Readers also will gain an understanding of the various components of a budget. The chapter concludes with a brief discussion of the critical accounting and financial reporting issues that influence budgets and budgeting.

Chapter 2 addresses the broader economic and political contexts of budgeting and describes the framework for the budgetary process—both on and off campus. The importance of enrollments as a major factor in terms of resources, expenses, and investments is highlighted, and the typical resources for independent and public institutions are examined. The chapter also analyzes the effects of various political and economic factors on institutional budgets. It explains how institutional resources are expended and describes the problems that arise when one attempts to apply traditional inflationary measures to higher education. Furthermore, given the shortcomings of more general inflationary measures, the chapter identifies alternative measures deemed more relevant to higher education.

The chapter also addresses critical policy issues—such as access, research priorities, and other demands on limited public resources—and how they affect institutional budgets. The impact of the state political environment is examined in terms of the availability of resources provided to public higher education.

Chapter 3 introduces the factors that shape a budget process and identifies the differences in processes used by various campuses. Role differentiation is discussed to provide a framework for understanding the perspectives different organizational levels offer within an institution. The capital budget and its relationship to the operating budget are explained. This chapter also provides examples of planning and budgeting cycles on different types of campuses. The discussion focuses on critical issues affecting the budgetary process, such as an institution's character and how it affects the role of faculty and academic administrators. It also speaks to the expectations created when one has the opportunity to participate in the budget process as well as the issues and factors that participants must consider.

Chapter 4 focuses on participants' roles as they seek to influence the operating and capital budgets. Specific budgetary approaches and characteristics are presented, including the need for flexibility, the process of linking budgeting to planning and measurement, and strategies for achieving budgetary objectives. A wide range of specific issues are examined, including how faculty salary adjustment pools are established; how faculty workload is measured; what factors are considered in making resource allocations; and what effect accounting requirements have on budget development.

Chapter 5 explores the sensitive issue of budgeting during extremely difficult fiscal situations—including retrenchment, potentially the most serious situation an institution might ever encounter. Although financial problems can arise at any time, certain economic conditions tend to increase the likelihood of serious problems. The current climate, though improving, is likely to stimulate more campuses to pursue strategies involving retrenchment. The discussion covers the importance of preparing for such occurrences rather than trying to address them while in the midst of a crisis, when the range of options is limited. The chapter provides strategies for addressing short-term, intermediate-term, and long-term problems. The discussion is equally relevant to both public and independent institutions.

It is not the objective of this book to address every possible budgeting variation that one might encounter. In fact, as with many things related to higher education, there may be as many different budget processes as there are institutions. The book seeks to identify the most important elements of the budgeting process and to provide the reader with information about the ways in which internal and external factors influence the budget.

The appendix explains the different budgetary approaches that an institution might apply. It addresses the most common higher education budgeting techniques, such as incremental and formula budgeting. It also describes budgeting techniques developed in governmental settings and applied by some institutions, such as zero-based budgeting, performance-based budgeting, and planning, programming, and budgeting systems. Finally, the appendix addresses newer budgeting strategies that appear to be gaining in popularity, such as responsibility center budgeting and initiative-based budgeting.

Every campus has a culture and an operating style that dictate how its budget is developed and which individuals—by title, role, responsibility, or personality—have the greatest influence over the final product. In some organizations—research institutions, for example—faculty voices may be heard loud and clear throughout the budget process. In other institutions—especially smaller, tuition-dependent institutions and many community colleges—the faculty may not be as actively involved in any aspect of the budget process. Traditions are important when dealing with something as sensitive as a budget process and everything it represents, but they should not be used as an excuse to justify "doing what we've always done." Effective budgeting provides a wonderful opportunity to review options and reprioritize an institution's agenda. Understanding the process for developing a budget, as well as the role an individual can play in that process, can have a significant impact on the future success of a campus.

chapter one

AN INTRODUCTION
TO BUDGETING

A budget is a map guiding an institution on its journey in pursuit of its mission. In most cases, the mission includes instruction, research, public service, and—in some cases—patient care. Regardless of the specific elements of an institution's mission, an effective budget will address them all. An astute observer should be able to learn a great deal about an organization merely by reviewing the budget. This process will suggest the relative importance of the mission components and detail how resources are expected to be received and how they will be expended.

Budgets take many forms, but they usually include at least two components: quantitative and narrative. The quantitative component is the most widely examined. It details the numbers that indicate the expected revenue—by category and by dollar level. It also provides the basic information about how funds will be expended. There are many different quantitative formats. Some are highly aggregated, showing just the major categories of revenues (e.g., tuition, investment income) and expenses (e.g., salaries and benefits, utilities). Others are very detailed, showing individual expense categories for specific organizational units.

The narrative component provides additional information about the various issues addressed in the quantitative budget. The narrative is especially helpful toward understanding what the budget represents. Depending on the budget model being used, the narrative may highlight the specific priorities addressed, the assumptions used in developing the budget, and the constraints that affect the numbers comprising the budget. It may also refer to specific goals and objectives for the organizational units at the institution.

Budgets serve many purposes and have various roles. At its most important level, the budget is the financial representation of the institution's plans. It is developed through iterative processes and, once finalized, presents the results of a multitude of resource allocation decisions. These decisions are not made in a vacuum. They reflect advice and guidance from the board, discussions among senior managers, and—in the most effective settings—dialogues involving the institution's various stakeholders. A budget must be linked to the institution's plans or it will not achieve the ultimate purpose of driving the institution toward enhanced service and improved quality.

The budget also serves as a contract between management and the operating units charged with carrying out the plans for the organization. The budget indicates what resources will be provided to the units and, in broad terms, what the units will focus on in utilizing those resources. Like many contracts, however, it does not represent a guarantee. Effective budgets include provisions for contingencies, but even considering these provisions, it is possible that unforeseen circumstances will prevent the organization from providing all the resources identified in the budget. Even so, it is important that both management and the units view the budget as a shared commitment.

Another aspect of the budget as a commitment is the role it plays as a control mechanism. Some organizations have sophisticated systems and processes to ensure that expenses are incurred in accordance with the budget. In these organizations, automated systems are designed to support line-item budgeting. In line-item budgeting, funds allocated for supplies must be spent for supplies, funds budgeted for travel can be used only for travel, and so on. In environments that use the budget for this type of control, transactions are not processed if they would result in deficits in the individual budget categories. In contrast, some organizations operate at a higher level of control. One such example might be an aggregate nonsalary expense pool. In this environment, specific budgets might not be established for supplies or travel. Instead, such expenses are charged against the nonsalary pool. Assuming that transactions are appropriately chargeable to the nonsalary pool, they are processed as long as funds are available.

Accountability is an alternative to a control environment. Rather than relying on preventing problems, an accountability environment grants authority and then charges responsible individuals with addressing problems that may arise. For instance, in the example above, the system controls likely would prevent a department from overspending its budget for travel. On the other hand, not allowing the department to process the transaction creates a different problem. Assuming the travel is essential for the department to fulfill its mission objectives, preventing the transaction from being processed also prevents the department from accomplishing the objectives. In a system relying on accountability, the transaction would be processed, and the department would be responsible for taking action to alleviate any resulting budget deficit. The responsible managers might need to request additional resources from the next unit up the organizational ladder, or they might simply transfer resources into the travel category from another category within the departmental budget.

Generally, the effort required to function in an environment of accountability is less than the effort needed to respond in a control environment. Because of the increased flexibility in accountability environments, less time is invested in administrative tasks related to small dollar transactions. It should be noted, however, that accountability environments work only when those granted budgetary authority operate in an effective manner and carry out their responsibilities as expected, or experience consequences for their failure to do so.

The travel scenario described above introduces another important aspect of budgeting. It highlights the reality that budgets rarely are completely accurate. At best, they represent an informed estimate of how things will unfold throughout the fiscal year. The actual results may differ significantly—at least at the detail level. To the extent that changes occur, a decision must be made whether to treat the change as a one-time event (e.g., travel to a conference that likely will not occur again) or something that should be reflected in future budgets on an ongoing basis (e.g., the decision to join an association with a requirement to pay annual dues). If the change has future implications, the budget process must include a mechanism for noting such events so they will be reflected when the next budget cycle begins.

The budget also is a forecast of the institution's financial picture at a future point in time. Assuming that a budget covers an annual operating cycle that coincides with the institution's fiscal year, the financial information in the budget can be used to generate pro forma financial statements. Such statements will depict the financial condition of the institution at the end of the cycle, assuming that the budget accurately reflects what will happen during the period on an aggregated basis. These statements are especially beneficial to an organization that has established a goal of achieving certain financial objectives along with its programmatic objectives.

Another role performed by the budget is that of an indicator of risk tolerance. As suggested earlier, numerous decisions must be made throughout the budget development process. Assumptions and predictions cover items as critical as the number of expected entering freshmen and transfer students and as mundane as the expected increase in elevator maintenance fees. Some decisions are imposed on the institution, such as increased utilities costs, while others are imposed by the institution, such as faculty salary increases. The specific decisions indicate the level of risk the institution can accommodate. The greater the risk tolerance, the less likely will be the contingencies built into the budget. Institutions with a high tolerance for risk will budget revenues aggressively and allocate nearly all resources for expenses (including appropriate additions to reserves for future uses, such as facilities maintenance). On the other hand, institutions that are less comfortable with risk are more likely to budget revenues conservatively and include contingency amounts to cover expenses that might not have been anticipated.

Finally, the budget is a political instrument. It reflects the outcome of a series of negotiations over which activities should be funded and at what levels. To create the budget, administrators from various units strike bargains and make tradeoffs. Many people seek to exert their leadership to influence the ultimate distribution of resources. It is typical for multiple budget cycles to be in operation at the same time, so it is common for negotiations in one cycle to influence other cycles. Although these negotiations rarely result in complete satisfaction for the parties involved, the process is worthwhile. The negotiations provide the opportunity to communicate needs for services and for the resources required to provide the services. This process can lead to a better understanding of other activities competing for the same scarce resources. Care is needed, though, because negotiations can be counterproductive if they are not properly managed. It is important that the process afford each perspective the opportunity to be heard and to receive feedback about the rationale for final decisions.

Budgeting Is an Iterative Process

All budgets are subject to revision. In fact, it is likely that the ink on the latest budget document will not be dry before circumstances dictate that adjustments be made. Even with the best of planning processes, some events and developments simply cannot be anticipated. In most cases, the budget for a given cycle begins with the budget from the previous cycle. Presumably, the starting point reflects the cumulative impact of all revisions to the previous budget—assuming they are not merely temporary situations—but even with this process, things will continue to change over time. The budget process and the budget itself must be flexible enough to respond to these changes.

Different organizations address the changes in different ways. For organizations that have budgeted revenues conservatively, positive net financial results may lead to increased allocations of resources for use in the current period. Similarly, organizations that include expense contingencies in the budget periodically will make adjustments to reallocate available resources from the contingency line to the category that has experienced an overrun. The number of budget adjustments tends to be lower for conservative organizations than for those that budget more aggressively. Aggressive budgeters often need to make more adjustments because they are more likely to experience revenue shortfalls and expense overruns. With luck, the net impact of the shortfalls and overruns will not create an overall deficit situation, but it is a possibility for organizations that rely on aggressive budget assumptions.

Why Bother With Budgeting?

Budgeting is a relatively recent phenomenon. Throughout much of recorded history, most activities were managed on a cash basis—especially in what now is thought of as the nonprofit sector. Activities and service levels varied based on the presence or absence of adequate resources. In the late 1800s public administration evolved to the point that there was a recognized need for effective planning and budgeting. Revenues were anticipated, and this information was used to develop expenditure plans. Budgets provided a mechanism for dealing with both known and anticipated financial problems in an organized manner. Even before the adoption of full accrual accounting, budgets proved incredibly valuable in eliminating the uncertainty that comes with pure cash accounting. Given that needs always exceeded resources, the advent of planning and budgeting helped organizations set priorities.

Even more than many other nonprofit organizations, colleges and universities have a very complex operating environment. The variety of revenue sources, the compliance requirements to which they are subject, and the nature of the restrictions attached to many of their resources make both planning and budget development challenging propositions. Still, without an effective budget process, managing a college or university from a financial perspective would be nothing less than chaos. An effective planning process leading to a clearly articulated budget provides a means of tracking revenues and expenses so that resources can be used most effectively to meet the institution's goals while still complying with external constraints.

Another important benefit provided by budgeting is the ability to highlight the costs of particular activities and their respective claim on resources. This exercise is especially valuable for activities supported with unrestricted resources. It is less necessary for activities supported with restricted resources because there usually is a direct linkage between revenues and expenses. If the revenues are reduced or eliminated, it is usually obvious that the activity will experience operational cutbacks or be terminated.

This scenario does not necessarily apply to activities supported by unrestricted resources because usually there is no direct link between the sources of revenues allocated to the activity and the activity's expenses. The budget provides a useful tool for articulating the activities that compete for unrestricted resources. When unrestricted resources are expected to increase, the organization has an opportunity to increase the resources allocated to particular activities, undertake new activities, or simply increase amounts reserved for future uses. These decisions become more evident when they are articulated through the budget.

Prelude to a Budget

In well-managed organizations, the budget is a manifestation of the organization's plans and reflects the relative priorities assigned to different activities. The important work related to financial decisions should be nearly complete before the budget process begins in earnest. Individual allocation decisions should grow from the decisions made throughout the planning process. It is almost too late to have a significant impact at the point that the budget is being developed.

The sad reality, however, is that relatively few higher education institutions have effective planning mechanisms, and even those that do, do not always integrate them with the budget process. In many instances, budgets are developed in incremental fashion, with the prior year's budget adjusted by a fixed percentage to address increases in spending. Although this approach is the most common, it generally will not enable an institution to achieve enhanced results, build on areas of strength, or steer the organization toward successful accomplishment of its mission.

Incremental processes do not lead to success because it is very unlikely that the current budget—the starting point—is allocated in the most optimal manner. Activities that might flourish with increased resources remain underfunded, while others that may have outlived their usefulness or value to the organization continue to consume resources. Incremental approaches are built on assumptions that the way resources currently are deployed is the most effective distribution; that all units have approximately equal needs for additional resources; and that maintaining the status quo is in the best interests of the institution. It is probably fair to say that another factor encouraging incrementalism is that it is the most efficient method. However, efficiency comes at the expense of effectiveness. The most successful approach to budgeting is to start with an effective plan—one developed with extensive input from all stakeholders—and to develop the budget based on the decisions reflected in the plan.

Types of Budgets

Higher education institutions use different budgets and variations of them for a number of purposes. The most pervasive form is the operating budget, the budget of greatest interest to the largest number of individuals. As its name suggests, this budget affects the most units in the institution. It covers all revenues and expenses that make up basic operations. It addresses the various components of the institution's mission, such as instruction and research, as well as supporting and ancillary activities, such as libraries and intercollegiate athletics.

Operating budgets identify all operating revenues—both those that result from various service efforts (for example, tuition, fees, and patient charges) and those derived from other sources (for example, governmental appropriations, gifts, and endowment income). The key consideration regarding operating budget revenues is that, with one exception, they all are used to provide the resources needed to finance the current expenses incurred by the organization's operating activities. The exception relates to reserves, which are a form of savings. The vast majority of revenues received during a given period will be expended during that period. The remaining, unexpended resources will be added to reserves—put aside for specific purposes, typically to be used in a future period. In some cases, however, reserves merely serve as a cushion against future financial problems. In these situations, it is hoped that it will never be necessary to expend the reserves.

In addition to revenues and reserves, operating budgets also address the day-to-day expenses incurred by the institution as it pursues its mission. Colleges and universities incur a wide variety of expenses. Some are pervasive, such as faculty salaries, and make up a very large percentage of the budget. Others may be relatively small and vary significantly based on the character of the institution. For instance, maintenance costs for residence halls typically are not a significant expense for community colleges.

Expenses in an operating budget may be displayed in either of two broad categories: natural classification or functional classification, sometimes called programmatic classification. Natural classification refers to expenses that are identified by type rather than purpose. Typical natural-class expenses include salaries, benefits, travel, and supplies. Though valuable for many purposes, a budget prepared using the natural classification approach provides very little information about the activities being conducted. For instance, the natural classification budget for a consulting firm might look very similar to one prepared for a research institute because both organizations are labor-intensive. A functional expense budget would be more valuable as an aid to understanding what is taking place.

Functional expenses are organized by the nature of the activity the expense supports. Typical functional categories for a college or university include instruction, public service, and academic support. Instructional expenses would consist of various natural-class expenses such as salaries, employee benefits, supplies, and travel. Similar expenses would occur in other functional categories.

A matrix displaying natural-class expenses in functional categories is a useful representation of the expense side of an operating budget. It provides a clear indication of the relative investments by functional category and indicates the proportional amount of various types of expenses incurred to achieve the various programmatic objectives.

Capital budgets are the next most common type of budget encountered on campuses. This budget maps out the finances for construction or other acquisition plans related to a campus's physical facilities and infrastructure. Like an operating budget, it addresses revenues, expenses, and reserves. The revenues can come from various sources, including tuition and fees, governmental appropriations, and gifts.

In addition to the resources provided by revenues, financing comes from two other sources: reserves and borrowing. Reserves are funds that have accumulated through savings or have been funded as part of the operating budget. Institutions often specify that a certain portion of the annual operating budget be set aside to cover costs that will be incurred in a future period. This practice is typical for auxiliary enterprise units, which must be self-supporting. For example, residence hall systems typically rely on borrowed funds to provide financing for new construction. It is a fairly standard requirement that a certain portion of annual system revenues be set aside for facilities maintenance such as carpet replacement, painting, and roof repairs. These funds are maintained in a reserve until they are needed.

Borrowed funds are either construction loans or long-term bonds that finance the acquisition or construction costs for new facilities, major equipment, or infrastructure upgrades or additions. The long-term debt serves the same purpose as a home mortgage for an individual. Colleges and universities frequently issue tax-exempt bonds, repayable over as many as 30 years, to fund capital expansion. For some public institutions, the bonds are issued by the state, or the state may provide the resources needed to repay the bonds as they come due.

Expenditures appearing in a capital budget include various construction costs (for example, amounts that will be capitalized) as well as other costs that, because they are not capitalizable, will be recognized as expenses during the current year.

Both operating and capital budgets can be developed for the institution as a whole or for subsets of the institution. For instance, a capital budget might apply to an individual project such as construction of a particular building, or it can address all approved capital projects. Similarly, operating budgets can address the complete range of activities for the institution, or they can simply cover activities within a department or school.

Special-Purpose Budgets

In addition to operating and capital budgets, several variations of budgets address specific situations. For instance, some organizations prepare special budgets focused only on restricted funds. Restricted resources are provided by external parties and carry stipulations about how they must be expended. Examples include gifts provided to acquire library books and income from an endowment established to fund scholarships for undergraduate students from a particular locale. Another example is a grant from a governmental entity that must be expended for specific purposes. Restricted budgets indicate resources and expenses for specific activities.

Accounting rules for restricted funds differ between public and independent institutions (see "Financial Reporting," below, and chapter 4). One difference affects the classification of resources as restricted or unrestricted. For independent institutions, only donors can create restricted resources. For public institutions, anyone outside the institution—including donors, creditors, and other governments—can create restrictions.

There are many other examples of special-purpose budgets employed by colleges and universities. The primary consideration is that they be clearly labeled and explained to avoid confusion about what they represent.

Financial Reporting

One need not be an accountant to understand budgets and budgeting. In some cases, knowledge of accounting may aid the understanding of relationships between various elements of a budget, but budgets as such are not subject to accounting rules. Nevertheless, some important accounting issues affect higher education budgeting. An awareness of them will be beneficial for those participating in or observing the budget process.

The most significant issue is the focus of the budget. Operating and capital budgets already have been touched on, and accounting drives some nuances for these budgets. A key difference between budgeting and accounting is that budgets usually focus on cash, while accounting considers cash activity as well as accruals. Accruals include revenues that have been earned but not collected in cash (receivables) and expenses that have been incurred but not paid for (payables).

Noncash expenses are a different type of accrual. Unlike payables, a noncash expense is a cost of doing business that must be recognized but that does not result in a current payment. The most common example is depreciation. Depreciation is the accounting mechanism used to spread the cost of capital assets, such as buildings and equipment, over the periods equating to their useful lives. Without this convention, funds expended to acquire high-cost assets would be charged entirely to the current year, automatically generating a financial loss. This approach ignores the reality that these assets will provide services far into the future. Instead, the amounts invested in the construction or acquisition of capital assets are recorded as assets rather than expenses. The useful life for such assets is estimated, and the value of the asset is divided by this number to generate an amount representing the annual charge for using or consuming a portion of the asset. This amount represents the expense (depreciation) attributable to each future period.

A key consideration in the treatment of depreciation is whether an attempt is made to generate revenues sufficient to offset the expense. In other words, are tuition and other revenue sources managed to cover all expenses or only cash expenses? The practice of generating revenues sufficient to cover both cash expenses and depreciation is referred to as funding depreciation. If this does not occur, noncash expenses like depreciation will cause the institution to report a financial loss each year.

There are mixed views on the issue of funding depreciation. Some professionals believe that it is necessary to recognize the expense of using facilities and establish reserves to provide for their replacement, despite the shortcomings of such an approach. Under current accounting practices, depreciation addresses only the original cost of a facility—or the estimated market value in the case of gifts. Obviously, this amount is far less than what might be needed to replace it 30 years in the future. Nevertheless, recognizing depreciation and covering the expense each year generates funds that can be invested with the objective of growing them sufficiently to cover most if not all of the replacement cost.

Other professionals argue that the institution is not likely to be required to generate the funds needed to replace facilities that wear out or become obsolete. They suggest that donors will be asked to provide these resources or, in the case of public institutions, government will provide the necessary funds. That may have been true for public institutions at one time, but it is becoming apparent that the current economic climate does not allow states to provide the resources needed to operate higher education, let alone finance asset replacement. Likewise, as facilities age or become obsolete, it will be even harder to find donors willing or able to provide the resources needed to maintain the physical infrastructure required by colleges and universities.

Another financial reporting issue with implications for budgeting is financial aid. Some forms of financial aid represent true inflows of resources to the institution, while others merely pass through the institution's accounts as they make their way to the students. Current accounting guidance dictates that revenues be considered only once. Until recently, colleges and universities counted revenues twice—once when the financial aid source was received and again, in the form of tuition, when the student registered. When financial aid was applied in satisfaction of the student's financial obligations, it was recognized as an expenditure—even though no money actually changed hands at that point.

Under current rules, revenues must be counted only once. If a form of financial aid is treated as revenue by the institution when it is received (for example, a gift for scholarships), the tuition for the student receiving the scholarship is reduced by the amount of gift applied as a scholarship. The net result is that both the gift and the balance of tuition paid by the student are recognized as revenues, and no expenditures or expenses are recognized for this transaction.

Despite the accounting requirements, it is important to consider tuition and financial aid as separate categories in the budget—even though they will likely be addressed at the same time due to the strong linkage between the two. It may be necessary to make adjustments when trying to reconcile the budget to the financial statements but, from a management perspective, tuition and financial aid are closely linked. Therefore, it is important to focus attention on the aggregate rather than the net amounts.

There is one other accounting issue to be considered when examining budgeting. It is an unfortunate reality that public institutions and independent institutions do not follow the same rules for financial reporting purposes. Independent institutions must comply with rules established by the Financial Accounting Standards Board, while public institutions are subject to rules developed by the Governmental Accounting Standards Board. Although the basic rules are similar, there are subtle differences between some of the standards that make it difficult to compare financial reports prepared by public and independent institutions. Although the differences have only limited impact on budgeting practices, their potential impact should be considered if one attempts to compare budgets for otherwise similar institutions.

chapter two

THE ECONOMIC AND POLITICAL ENVIRONMENT

An institution's budget is subject to general economic and political influences. Most external forces are beyond the control of individual institutions or even the national higher education community. Accordingly, budgeters must anticipate changes in economic and political conditions that may affect the amount of revenues available and, of equal importance, the expenses the institution may have to bear. Unless an institution's budget can withstand the pressures created by external forces, its survival may be in jeopardy.

The economic changes experienced by higher education during the last several decades have had significant effects on institutions. In many respects, the turmoil of the recent past reflects a sea change in the nation's support for higher education. Higher education no longer enjoys the high ranking on national, state, and local societal agendas that it once held. There is ample evidence to suggest that other sectors are capturing resources that previously were directed to higher education, especially in terms of governmental support. Whether the focus is security, K-12 education, health care, or general social service programs, it is apparent that higher education no longer is viewed as a top priority. Part of this shift stems from a change in perception. Instead of viewing higher education as a public good, some see it as a private benefit, and others see it as an entitlement.

In today's environment higher education must defend itself continuously against criticism from numerous quarters. In years past it was enough to highlight the value of a college education in economic terms or point to the discoveries growing out of campus-based research. Such arguments no longer sway a nation that no longer focuses on ability to pay. The issue has shifted to a willingness to pay. As college prices have escalated—outpacing inflation in most years—both the federal government and the general population have questioned whether higher education is being managed effectively.

The current economic climate is one of the toughest in decades. Although inflation has been held in check, campuses still are experiencing cost increases in critical areas. At the same time, various revenue sources are depressed, and there is nothing to suggest that things will turn around in the short run. In fact, even prestigious institutions have been forced to suspend programs, eliminate positions, or resort to other cost-cutting measures that have dramatic effects on program delivery. In a climate like this one, external factors must be examined even more carefully.

The National Economic Environment

The economies of all institutions are linked with the national economy, which is increasingly connected to the world economy. Some of these macroeconomic issues set the boundaries for the economies of institutions. The purpose of this chapter is not to provide a primer on macroeconomics or to suggest what the economic future will hold, except in the broadest possible terms. Instead, the primary goal is to highlight some of the relationships between the national economy and institutional policy and to suggest that the impact of the national economy is likely to become more significant in the future.

If this book were being written just a few years ago, this section would have a very different tone. The national economy was strong, savings levels were up, financial markets were performing at all-time highs, national productivity was rising comfortably on an annual basis, and the federal budget was generating a surplus for the first time in years. Except for some concerns about tuition prices during the mid- to late 1990s, higher education was experiencing a relatively comfortable period. Enrollments were up, and endowments were growing, both as a result of investment performance and significantly increased giving levels. Public support was at an all-time high.

The economic environment has changed dramatically since then. The federal budget deficit is once again on the rise, and the trade deficit grows larger each year. Financial markets are unsettled, and though there are modest signs of recovery, markets and indexes remain far below the levels of the late 1990s. All these factors, coupled with the United States' current involvement in two wars, have created an economic situation that is, at best, of significant concern to higher education. Resources diverted to pay for defense, security, or interest on the national debt are not available to support higher education research or student financial aid.

Unless there is a dramatic turnaround fairly soon, higher education will face a rocky road for the foreseeable future. The concern about college costs appears to be resurfacing and intensifying. In the late 1990s Congress took a strong interest in the pricing decisions made by many campuses and the impact they had on those seeking advanced education. In response to annual tuition increases significantly above inflation levels, Congress created the National Commission on the Cost of Higher Education to explore the situation.

For the better part of a year, the commission conducted analyses and heard testimony about the economic situation in higher education. The outcomes were somewhat mixed. On the one hand, the commission recommended no specific actions that would have harmed institutions or the industry. On the other hand, it chastised the industry for not doing enough to hold down costs and for not being more forthcoming about tuition pricing decisions and higher education finances generally. The commission's report, *Straight Talk About College Costs and Prices*,[1] provided a valuable public service by defining several key terms that had been used interchangeably during the tuition debate.

Costs: What institutions spend to provide education and related educational services to students.

Price: What students and their families are charged and what they pay.

General Subsidy: The difference between the costs to the institution of providing an education and the tuition and fees charged to students.[2]

The report highlights the fact that almost every student attending an independent or public institution receives a general subsidy, while a substantial number also receive specific subsidies in the form of financial aid.

The report also refers to the "opaque relationship between costs and prices." While acknowledging that there are significant cost drivers affecting the prices institutions charge, the report criticizes higher education for not being rigorous in its attempts to understand the relationship between costs and prices. It further charges that because institutions do not attempt to understand their financial structures, they are not able to be more transparent with their finances. Even those within an institution find it difficult to understand its financial structure, and only minimal effort is invested in educating the public about these matters.

Although various groups, including NACUBO, have attempted to respond to the commission's recommendations, not enough has been done. In fact, during the deliberations on the 2004 reauthorization of the Higher Education Act, Republican legislators attempted to implement a form of price control on colleges, although it was not labeled as such. The proposed legislation would have imposed various sanctions on campuses found to have raised tuition at what Congress deemed excessive levels during a specified period. The ultimate sanction would have resulted in a reduction of federal financial aid available to the offending institution's students. The legislation did not pass, but Congress continues to pressure institutions to justify price increases that exceed what is believed to be reasonable. It is generally anticipated that continuing increases in tuition will draw increased attention from the federal government. It doesn't help the situation that the average price increase at public institutions was 10.5 percent during 2004–05 and 14 percent during 2003–04.[3] For these two years the trend is in the right direction, but the overall rate of increase remains high by historical standards. Part of the problem stems from a reduction in support from the states. Public institutions' costs continue to increase, partially because of increased enrollment, yet the states have cut back on appropriations in recent years. Although Congress acknowledges this situation, they seem more interested in pressuring colleges and universities than in taking direct action against the states. As a result, institutions are forced to take the only remedy available to them: increase tuition.

Revenues represent only one side of the equation. Costs are a significant consideration. Many institutions have taken steps to control their costs. Quality improvement and efficiency initiatives have helped in some isolated instances, but the fact remains that it is expensive to deliver quality education. The range of costs faced by a campus is far-reaching, starting with people. Higher education is a labor-intensive industry. Current staffing models result in some campuses spending in excess of 70 percent of their total budgets on compensation. In addition to faculty and others directly related to the academic mission, the regulatory environment in which higher education operates requires numerous administrative and support positions.

Another significant cost category is facilities. Higher education is also a capital-intensive industry, with huge costs invested in facilities construction and maintenance. Utilities represent a significant operating cost, even for campuses in temperate climates. For many institutions, facilities costs are incurred around the clock. The range of services provided to support the primary missions of instruction, research, and public service extends to auxiliary units serving students 24 hours a day.

Second only to health insurance, the fastest-growing cost category for campuses is technology. As society becomes more dependent on technology, institutions must keep pace—both to meet their own needs and to teach the most current technologies. Massive amounts have been invested in administrative software to enable institutions to manage effectively. For some, technology is an alternative to hiring more staff to conduct the institution's business. For others, however, the technology actually creates increased staffing demands. Because the newer technologies are so sophisticated and bring increased capabilities, it is not uncommon to have to increase the investment in personnel to maintain and gain maximum benefit from the technology. Finally, the cost of regulation continues to rise. The federal government is the worst offender in this regard, but the state can also add to the problem for public institutions.

When one examines selected aggregate statistics about higher education, it becomes a little easier to comprehend the magnitude of the industry. As of 2003, there were 4,168 degree-granting institutions in the United States.[4] The latest year for which aggregate expenditure data are available is fiscal year 2000. During that year total expenditures reached $291 billion,[5] representing 2.9 percent of the nation's gross domestic product. These funds were expended in support of 15.9 million students enrolled in full-time and part-time degree programs.[6] Off-campus extension, noncredit continuing education, and community service programs reached many millions more. Higher education institutions employed 3.1 million individuals during fall 2001, two-thirds of whom were full-time. Of the total employment, the largest single category—as one would hope—is faculty, amounting to 1.1 million employees. The next largest category, consisting of 957,000 employees and identified as nonprofessionals in the U.S. Department of Education's data collection, includes clerical personnel, custodians, skilled trades, and a variety of other job classifications. The remaining positions fall into various nonfaculty professional categories, including senior administrators (such as presidents, chancellors, and provosts), accountants, planners, and institutional researchers.[7]

An enterprise as large as higher education is affected by the same economic and political pressures that affect other major social programs. Some of the most significant pressures are long-term: human resource costs, especially in such a labor-intensive industry; the costs of facilities maintenance; the prices of purchased goods and services, especially specialty items such as journal subscriptions and research equipment; the costs of complying with federal and other sponsor regulations; and reduced federal aid and state support as policy makers seek to manage deficits generated by a stagnant economy.

Human Resource Costs

By a wide margin, the largest single expense category in higher education is compensation—salaries, wages, and benefits. For some institutions, compensation can represent as much as 75 percent of total expenses. The labor-intensive nature of higher education poses real problems for those responsible for developing budgets. The major difficulty is that the educational model does not lend itself to dramatic gains in productivity. Increased productivity in higher education is defined as an increase in the value of services without a corresponding increase in costs. Some service industries, particularly financial services, have employed technology to achieve significant gains in productivity without raising overall costs. Technology, though essential to conducting activities in higher education, provides only marginal improvement in productivity. Many operate under the mistaken belief that the introduction of instructional technology can dramatically increase the number of students taught by a single faculty member. There clearly are unique situations in which a single faculty member—either via large lectures or Web-based instruction—can serve large numbers of students. For the most part, however, low student-faculty ratios are deemed to produce the most effective outcomes. A true gain in productivity requires that the quality of the service remain at comparable levels. Thus, larger classes will not increase a faculty member's productivity unless the quality of instruction is maintained.

With such a large proportion of the costs in a labor-intensive industry being personnel related, the only way to achieve significant economies through means other than productivity is to control salaries or benefits. When resources remain flat or decline, average compensation or the number of employees must decline, or deficits will develop. Institutions that anticipate financial difficulties and plan accordingly will have more options available, and should have fewer traumatic experiences, than institutions that do not manage their finances effectively.

It is not always possible to avoid financial difficulties because so many events are beyond the control of the institution. On the other hand, it is always possible to prepare for the possibility by developing plans in advance of the problem. Even when plans are in place, serious financial difficulties almost always result in staffing reductions. There are various ways to accomplish this, however. With appropriate planning, normal attrition (for example, retirements and resignations) may be a viable option that enables an institution to avoid involuntary terminations when relatively small savings are needed. If large-scale savings are needed, involuntary personnel actions are inevitable, but care must be taken. Cutting faculty and staff positions will dramatically affect morale—especially if done over a short period. Moreover, rapid workforce reductions are difficult to accomplish in higher education because of tenure and contracts. Achieving savings through attrition clearly is more humane, but it may not be a feasible option during difficult economic conditions. The message here is that institutions should ensure that plans are in place to deal with personnel actions well in advance of the need to implement them. Planning for such an eventuality before the crisis hits enables one to make informed decisions without facing the pressure of the moment. (See chapter 5 on responding to extraordinary financial difficulties.)

Higher education is facing a difficult period in terms of resources and costs—especially in human resources. This challenge is occurring at a time when many members of the baby boom generation are approaching traditional retirement age yet choosing to postpone retirement. Ten years ago it was estimated that 45 to 50 percent of faculty were age 50 or older.[8] That percentage is believed to have increased significantly. Because of the recent poor performance of the financial markets, many people saw their investment portfolios take major hits. As a result, many faculty and other employees are electing to continue working in order to contribute more to their retirement programs and to allow the programs to recover ground lost during the early part of the decade. With the economy remaining relatively stagnant, it is possible that institutions experiencing severe financial difficulties will be forced to take extreme measures to achieve the savings needed to balance budgets.

Readers are cautioned not to focus excessively on salaries and wages without devoting adequate attention to benefits, which represent a significant expense category. Some benefits provide current protection for employees or their families, such as workers' compensation; health, life, and disability insurance; and even unemployment compensation. Others provide protection for the employee once he or she retires. These benefits include Social Security, pensions, and postretirement benefits such as health insurance. The cumulative investment in these benefits is substantial. Institutions used to bear the full cost, especially independent institutions, but now it is much more common for employees to pay a share. Health insurance premiums, which frequently were paid fully by the employer, now are shared. Similarly, many institutions have converted their pension plans from defined-benefit—under which the institution was obligated to contribute enough funds to guarantee a specified level of retirement benefits based on age and service—to defined-contribution. The latter approach specifies the amount of current contribution required of the employer but does not guarantee a specific level of benefit. The combination of these changes—coupled with the increasing popularity of options for individuals to contribute directly to their retirement savings through individual retirement accounts, 401(k) (income deferral) plans, and 403(b) (tax-sheltered annuity) plans, has resulted in employees bearing more of the cost than ever. Nevertheless, benefits are a significant expense category that must be examined periodically to determine whether it requires adjustment.

Facilities Maintenance and Related Costs

Most institutions invested heavily in physical plant to accommodate increased enrollments during the 1960s, 1970s, and 1980s. More recently, additional investments were made for two reasons. First, resources became available as a result of the significant increase in endowment performance and private giving. Second, many institutions chose improving the physical plant as a strategy for enhancing their competitiveness in student and faculty recruitment. Recent investments focused in several areas, including recreational facilities, research facilities, and upgraded classroom facilities.

Since the significant shift in the economic climate, investment in new facilities has been curtailed dramatically. In fact, in many instances, campuses were barely able to complete projects undertaken before the downturn. Some projects were abandoned, causing the institutions to experience a loss on their investments.

There never is a good time to experience financial problems, but from a facilities standpoint, the current downturn may have come at the worst possible time. Facilities built during the second half of the twentieth century are nearing the end of their useful lives and therefore require disproportionately high investments in repairs and maintenance. As of 1995 (the most current data available), the cumulative backlog of deferred maintenance in higher education totaled $26 billion. More than 20 percent of campuses had a backlog of $15 million or greater, with public institutions having the biggest problem.[9] Even relatively new construction poses a problem because, if not maintained properly, the cost of operating these facilities will increase substantially in a very short time.

This situation is particularly alarming because postponing needed maintenance is a common practice on many campuses. As budgets are squeezed, it becomes more difficult to meet all operating expenses. Because many facets of facilities maintenance are invisible to the average person, it becomes relatively easy for senior administrators to elect to postpone needed investments. This problem compounds because, in addition to not making the investments required today, the facilities not being maintained adequately will deteriorate more rapidly. Some institutions make no provisions for maintaining facilities, although others have established policies in recent years that prohibit the addition of new facilities unless adequate resources are identified to maintain the new facilities. Although this approach will affect future maintenance needs, it does nothing to address the backlog. There are no standards for the amount that should be invested in ongoing facilities maintenance, but institutions that invest 1.2 to 1.7 percent of a facility's replacement value to cover routine repair and maintenance should be able to avoid serious problems.

Another contributing factor is the need to renew and/or upgrade facilities to take advantage of newer technologies. With the ubiquity of technology in every facet of college and university operations and activities, nearly every campus facility must be connected to the Internet through hard wiring or wireless technology, and every classroom must accommodate the use of technology in instructional activities. The addition of this capability represents a significant cost, but without these investments institutions will have trouble scheduling classes to meet the instructional needs of their faculty.

Technology Costs

One of the fastest growing expense categories in higher education is technology. It is difficult to obtain reliable expenditure data for technology because so much of the investment is made from decentralized budgets. It is estimated, however, that approximately 7 percent of total campus spending is devoted to computing and other forms of information technology.[10] Total spending for academic computing—devoted primarily to instructional technology and faculty research—represents one-third of the total technology investment. Whether considered in terms of the costs of implementing administrative applications such as enterprise resource planning systems—which can run into the tens of millions of dollars—or the introduction of technology into the classroom, technology is not inexpensive.

Technology has multiple facets, and their cost patterns vary significantly. Hardware costs have declined significantly over time, so that almost any item, whether a personal computer or a cell phone, costs less today than it did even a year ago. This statement can be misleading, though, because most people are not satisfied with replacing their existing technology with comparable technology. If a computer wears out or becomes obsolete, users seek a faster and more powerful model with increased functionality—and higher cost, though significantly enhanced capability for the user. Similarly, today's software comes with vastly enhanced power but higher price tags. Then there is the people side of the equation. Institutions are finding that, even when they can gain some control over hardware and software costs, they may not be able to do the same with the cost of technology workers. The decade of the 1990s in particular was a difficult time for those seeking to manage their investment in technology staff. Salaries were booming, and programmers, analysts, and engineers could double their salaries within a few years if they were willing to "job hop." Technology workers were demanding and receiving huge salaries as well as stock options. Higher education was not in a position to provide stock options and, in many cases, was unable to offer competitive salaries. The late 1990s found campuses fully consumed with preparing to operate in the new millennium. To deal with the Y2K problem, campuses scrambled to purchase and implement new systems or convert existing systems to accept a four-digit year code.

The situation came under some control in the early part of this decade. A major factor was the burst of the so-called technology bubble, which had grown in the late 1990s as various dotcom companies were established and drew huge investment dollars.

The reliance on technology is not going to diminish. In fact, it is likely to increase dramatically. For instance, a relatively untapped market involves Web-enabled distance education. Current data on the possible impact are not available but, between 1997–98 and 2000–01, the number of students enrolled in distance-education courses more than doubled, from 1.3 million to 2.9 million. More than half of all institutions were offering distance-education courses by 2000–01, including nearly 90 percent of public institutions.[11]

Increased Cost of Purchased Goods and Services

To track price changes, higher education relied for many years on the Higher Education Price Index (HEPI) as an alternative to the more popular Consumer Price Index (CPI). The CPI was deemed too general and not representative of the types of purchases made by higher education institutions. The HEPI was thought to be more appropriate because the so-called market basket of goods was constructed to be more representative of higher education's typical purchases. The HEPI considers faculty and staff salaries; the prices of contracted services such as telecommunications and transportation; and the prices for supplies and materials, equipment, books and periodicals, and utilities. The categories are weighted in HEPI based on their relative importance in an institution's budget, after excluding sponsored research.

The HEPI has not been without its critics, and it no longer represents the standard for higher education price changes. One reason that HEPI never enjoyed universal acceptance stems from the fact that it was developed in the private sector. There also were questions about the validity of the method used to calculate the index. Because of these issues, there have been various attempts to identify an appropriate price index. Other than HEPI, the most frequently used index in recent years is the CPI-U. This index is a variation of the CPI in that it is based on goods and services purchased by the typical urban consumer. Some argue that, because HEPI and the CPI-U have not differed dramatically for some brief periods, the CPI-U is a reasonable choice. Others contend that, over time, significant variances can occur. As a result, efforts continue to identify a reliable index for use by higher education.

Recent efforts by the State Higher Education Executive Officers (SHEEO) ultimately may provide the best solution. In *State Higher Education Finance FY 2003*,[12] SHEEO presents a sound argument in support of a new index, the Higher Education Cost Adjustment (HECA). The index is constructed using two existing indexes, both maintained by the federal government. The first, the Employment Cost Index (ECI), is particularly relevant to higher education because it focuses on salaries and benefits for private-sector white-collar workers, exclusive of sales occupations. Given the labor-intensive nature of higher education and its preponderance of white-collar workers, this index is an appropriate one to include. Because higher education's costs do not consist exclusively of salaries, however, a second index must be added to the mix. SHEEO selected the Gross Domestic Price Implicit Price Deflator (GDP IPD). The GDP is the total market value of all final goods and services produced in the nation during a given year. Although not specific to higher education, its broad applicability and the wide range of products and services utilized by institutions, makes it an appropriate index to include. The Implicit Price Deflator is the component of the GDP IPD that converts the annual measure to an inflation index. The weighting of the respective indexes is 75 percent ECI and 25 percent GDP IPD, which reflects the historical distribution of expenses in higher education between salaries and other expenses. It is anticipated that the HECA will prove useful to institutions and others seeking to measure the impact of inflation on higher education finances.

Analysis using HECA demonstrates that costs in higher education have risen more rapidly than those in the general economy. Based on SHEEO data, which establishes 1990 as a base year, the CPI-U rose to 140.34 by 2002.[13] For the same period, HECA increased to 148.83. This inflation rate is not nearly as troubling as what was experienced in earlier decades—particularly the early 1970s during the first oil crisis and the 1980s, when interest rates rose to unprecedented levels. Nevertheless, prices are increasing and will continue to do so—especially as defense spending continues to increase.

Although steadily increasing prices can be accommodated through effective planning and cost management, most institutional budgets cannot withstand major fluctuations over short periods. Furthermore, exceptional cost increases in any category can wreak havoc on even a well-managed budget. For instance, colleges and universities continually face the prospect of replacing expensive instructional and research equipment as it becomes obsolete. Unless institutions have funded depreciation and maintained reserves for this purpose, the depreciation impact from these purchases will be a significant charge on the current budget and may have significant cash flow impacts as well. Depending on the magnitude of this problem for a given campus, the impact on the budget can be severe. Similar exceptional situations will force colleges and universities to deal with serious financial crises.

Costs of Federal Regulation and Social Programs[*]

A portion of the costs of doing business in any industry can be attributed to informal social pressures and government mandates in a number of areas: personal security and safety, participation and due process, public information, and environmental projection to name a few. Colleges and universities experience costs associated with these universal pressures and with several peculiar to higher education: protection of students' privacy, federal grants and contracts, teaching hospitals and clinics, and federal financial aid programs. Federal regulations and mandated social programs touch all aspects of institutional operations, from athletics to the care of laboratory animals.

It has proven to be difficult, if not impossible, to isolate the true cost of externally imposed regulations and guidelines. A primary reason is that compliance with the mandates often cannot be separated from the routine operations of the institution. Another reason is that colleges and universities frequently support the objectives of imposed regulations and programs and, even without the requirements, would initiate similar actions on their own.

The following factors must be considered in assessing the impact of federal regulation and social pressures:

- ◆ The adoption of programs can result in increased or decreased costs. For example, a mandated staff training program may lead to greater employee morale and improved productivity, thereby reducing operating costs.

- ◆ The costs of socially imposed programs must be considered in two parts: the costs of program operations and the costs associated with compliance (for example, reporting). In many cases, the concern about program costs is focused on the compliance aspects rather than the substance of the program.

---

[*] This section is based largely on Howard Bowen, *The Costs of Higher Education: How Much Do Colleges and Universities Spend per Student and How Much Should They Spend?* (San Francisco: Jossey-Bass, 1980).

- How costs are counted and when they must be incurred introduce another set of issues. The overall costs of a program may not be significant when measured over time. Too often, however, the mandate requires significant upfront investments that become a burden on a single year's budget.

- The implementation of some programs may not result in an increase in aggregate expenses but may force a shift in priorities. For instance, resources once earmarked for library acquisitions may be diverted to cover safety and security mandates.

Overall, for-profit entities have an advantage in dealing with socially imposed costs. First, because they do not typically receive federal funding, many regulations do not apply to them. In addition, when they are subject to external mandates that result in increased operating costs, they can pass these costs along to their customers. Although independent institutions have control of their tuition, this is not always the case for public institutions. Frequently, a state agency or the legislature has the authority to set tuition at public institutions. When institutions are unable to raise tuition to offset the costs of mandated programs, the only option is to cut back in other areas—either in the primary programs of instruction, research, and public service or in a support activity.

Some of the mandates and requirements applicable to higher education are summarized below to provide a sense of the complexities and range of issues campuses must address.

Personal security and safety. Examples of federal laws and regulations that affect higher education include the Social Security Act of 1935, as amended, addressing retirement pensions, survivors' benefits, disability insurance, unemployment compensation, and health insurance; the Occupational Safety and Health Act of 1970 (OSHA), establishing employee safety and working condition standards; the Employee Retirement Income Security Act of 1974 (ERISA), providing safeguards for employees participating in pensions offered by independent institutions; legislation on radiation safety and the protection of human and animal subjects used in research and teaching; and the 1999 Department of Education regulations mandating the reporting of campus crime statistics.

Working condition standards. Major laws include the National Labor Relations Act of 1935, establishing the rules applicable to collective bargaining and employee organizing; the Fair Labor Standards Act of 1938, establishing minimum wage levels, maximum work hours, and overtime compensation rules; and the Equal Pay Act of 1963, mandating that employees doing similar tasks must receive equal pay regardless of sex.

Personal opportunity. Although various courts have reduced protections in some areas related to affirmative action, guidelines remain in force through federal regulations and laws, including Executive Order 11246 of 1965, as amended in 1967, prohibiting discrimination on the basis of sex; the Employment Act of 1967, prohibiting discrimination on the basis of age; Title VII of the Civil Rights Act of 1964, as amended by the Equal Employment Opportunity Act of 1972, prohibiting discrimination on the basis of sex, race, creed, or national origin; Title IX of the Educational Amendments of 1972, prohibiting discrimination on the basis of sex in educational policies, facilities, programs, and employment practices; student financial aid programs rules, some of which require institutional contributions and, in all cases, impose significant administrative burdens; Internal Revenue Service regulations concerning discrimination in favor of highly compensated individuals and in student admissions; and various judicial decisions.

Participation, openness, due process, and privacy. The guiding legislation includes the First Amendment to the Constitution; the National Labor Relations Act of 1935; and the Family Educational Rights and Privacy Act of 1974 (FERPA, or the Buckley Amendment), dealing with the management of records and the release of information. More recent legislation, the Gramm-Leach-Bliley Act, aimed at financial institutions, imposes requirements to protect the privacy of consumers engaging in financial transactions. Colleges and universities originally were thought to be exempt from the rules, but the Federal Trade Commission issued regulations that extend aspects of the act to campuses. More recently, terrorist actions and threats have clouded the issues related to privacy, with the result that campuses frequently are caught in the middle in terms of attempting to comply with FERPA while responding to requests for information from various federal agencies.

Public information. Requests for information occur primarily in six areas: consumer protection, fund raising, enforcement of government programs, general statistical needs of society, national security, and general public demands for accountability. Examples include the need to clear with the

Office of Management and Budget (OMB) all surveys to be funded under federal grants; the financial, faculty and staff effort, and other reporting requirements under OMB Circular A-21, dictating the procedures for calculating facilities and administrative (F&A) cost rates applicable to sponsored activities; verification and audit reports on federally funded student financial aid participation; and the annual data collection through the Department of Education's National Center for Education Statistics Integrated Postsecondary Education Data System (IPEDS). One of the newest and most challenging examples in this area is the Student and Exchange Visitor Information System (SEVIS). SEVIS is an outgrowth of the tragic events of September 11, 2001. The Web-based system, a program of U.S. Immigration and Customs Enforcement, requires that all colleges and universities provide information on international students, scholars, and other visitors.

Environmental protection. Colleges and universities are increasingly affected by pollution control requirements, restrictions on research involving hazardous materials and recombinant DNA, and vandalism and the problems of neighborhood deterioration. Examples include a variety of laws administered by the Environmental Protection Agency, which has imposed stiff fines on campuses in recent years. Fines have been assessed under the Resource Conservation and Recovery Act, mandating specific safety steps related to the treatment of hazardous waste; the Toxic Substances Control Act, mandating storage and usage procedures for industrial chemicals; and several other acts.

Disabilities. The Americans with Disabilities Act of 1990 specifies requirements for making programs and facilities accessible to persons with disabilities. The act also requires that employers make accommodations to enable those with disabilities to participate in various activities, including employment, education, and commercial activities.

Shared costs in federal grants and contracts. Institutions are expected to absorb some of the costs associated with conducting research sponsored through federal grants and contracts. Cost sharing occurs in several ways. First, a statutory requirement is imposed on institutions receiving funding from federal sponsors such as the National Science Foundation and the National Institutes of Health. Institutions must expend nonfederal resources equal to a specified percentage of federal awards received to supplement amounts received from federal sponsors.

It was once common practice for federal agencies to expect campuses to propose voluntary cost sharing levels with grant applications submitted in response to requests for proposals. The effect was to force institutions to compete for awards based on the amount they were willing to spend to obtain the award rather than on the merits of the research proposal. However, federal sponsors have now discontinued the practice.

One cost issue that remains an ongoing source of frustration for campuses results from the federal government's approach to the reimbursement of facilities and administrative (F&A) costs related to sponsored activity. OMB Circular A-21 contains a complex set of requirements. In theory, the purpose of the calculation mandated under A-21 is to assure that the government and the institution pay their respective fair shares of the direct and indirect costs of sponsored projects. In recent years, however, the government has disallowed particular cost categories completely and imposed seemingly arbitrary caps on others. The net result of these actions is to force campuses to bear an increasingly larger share of the F&A costs of conducting research.

Moreover, the government has imposed additional requirements that increase the amount of unreimbursed costs by incorporating the provisions of the Cost Accounting Standards Board (CASB) in A-21. The CASB standards were designed to address issues in the for-profit defense contracting industry. Many of the provisions do not recognize the uniqueness of the nonprofit approach taken by colleges and universities. One particularly burdensome requirement applies to institutions that receive the largest amount of federal sponsored support. These institutions must make a comprehensive filing with the federal government, the DS-2 Disclosure Statement, describing their accounting practices in significant detail.

Management practices and audit standards. Institutions receiving federal support in the form of student financial aid or sponsored grants and contracts are subject to rules promulgated by the sponsoring agencies as well as by OMB. OMB Circular A-110 specifies uniform administrative requirements applicable to all federal programs. OMB Circular A-133, the single-audit standard, specifies the requirements for audits of federally funded programs and activities. In theory, the standard should assure that colleges and universities undergo only one annual federal financial audit. All federal agencies are expected to rely on that audit process to assure that their resources were managed appropriately. In practice, however, many federal agencies elect to go beyond the requirements of A-133 and conduct their own audits.

Special costs of teaching hospitals and clinics. Teaching hospitals and clinics are subject to restrictions and guidelines governing patient care review, patient privacy, accreditation and licensure, accounting procedures, control and care of drugs and blood, use of radiation, and use of human and animal subjects for research purposes. Early in this decade, concerns related to the safety and informed consent of human subjects used in research protocols (for instance, drug studies) led to temporary suspensions of thousands of projects under way at numerous teaching hospitals affiliated with medical schools. The Office for Protection from Research Risks of the National Institutes of Health suspended human subjects research at many institutions as a result of inadequacies found in the operation of institutional review boards, the campus groups charged with assuring that research protocols satisfy various guidelines. More recently, Congress passed the Health Insurance Portability and Accountability Act (HIPAA), which has a dramatic impact on all colleges and universities. Although primarily targeted to hospitals and physicians serving the general public, HIPAA imposes significant burdens on higher education student health and counseling clinics to assure the privacy and security of patient information.

Demographic Considerations

The demographic profile of the United States profoundly affects higher education institutions. Although the historical emphasis has been on the traditional college-age population (18 to 24 years old), recent trends indicate that nontraditional students are becoming a more significant factor in enrollments. This always has been true for two-year institutions, but it is becoming more a reality for four-year institutions as well.

Enrollments have risen steadily in recent years, and the trend is expected to continue. Based on Department of Education data, enrollment totaled 15.3 million in 2000 and will grow to between 17.5 million and 18.1 million students by 2010. The enrollment growth will be relatively evenly distributed between traditional college-age students and others. During 2000, approximately 61 percent of all students in degree-granting institutions were traditional college-age students. By 2010, based on the median range projections, nontraditional students will decrease from 39 percent of the total to 37.5 percent—assuming that current patterns continue.[14] The population size of traditional college-age students, from which enrollments in 2010 will come, is known today. Barring dramatic changes in immigration patterns, or in the percentage of these students pursuing college, the projections are likely to hold true.

The potential population of nontraditional students, however, has a significant likelihood for positive fluctuations for two reasons. First, the size of the potential nontraditional student population is substantially larger as a percentage of the total population. Second, and possibly more importantly, employers' expectations are such that advanced education is becoming a requirement. Although not all nontraditional students pursue degrees, more of them will be seeking advanced training and education. Colleges and universities have identified this potential growth area, and it is likely that they will be successful in capturing this market.

Changing demographics will affect different regions and types of institutions in different ways. Most institutions recruit on a regional basis. Therefore, trends among high school graduates are an important determinant of what may happen at the college level. A range of factors has caused the numbers of high school graduates to vary by region. Of greatest significance is the population migration generally from the North to the South and West. The South continues to have the largest school-age population, followed by the West, which recently outpaced the Midwest. The Northeast brings up the rear in terms of current K–12 enrollment. As the movement of the West into the second spot suggests, trends in enrollment growth are shifting. The South will see the largest growth in enrollments, totaling nearly 850,000 students—an increase of approximately 5.3 percent—between 2001–02 and 2007–08. The West also will see an increase of 365,000 more students, representing a 3.2 percent change. On the other hand, both the Midwest and the Northeast will see a net decline in the number of enrolled students during this period. The Midwest will lose more than 100,000 students, representing just under 1 percent of their current enrollments, while the Northeast will lose 250,000 students, a 2.6 percent decline. Shifts of this type, which affect the number of high school graduates, have significant implications for the institutions in those regions—especially those that are tuition dependent.[15]

As a result of the changing demographic profile, most colleges and universities will continue to engage in intense competition for students. Competition in regions with declining school-age populations will become more intense. Even institutions that are not seeking to increase enrollments will attempt to improve the overall quality of their student bodies. Institutions will increase the amounts invested in institutional student aid, and they will have to examine carefully the menu of offerings made available. As higher education has adopted a more customer-friendly attitude, institutions have modified approaches by offering classes at times more convenient to students, shifting to Web delivery for some programs and courses, and pursuing transfer students more aggressively.

Change in Federal Funding Philosophy

The 1990s were a generous period for higher education—especially in terms of research funding. The major funding agencies all saw significant increases in their budgets throughout the latter part of the decade, and this change translated into substantial growth in sponsored funding. Federally funded student financial aid also increased dramatically, although there remained a significant amount of unmet need. Still, it is likely that we will look back on this period as one of the golden eras of federal support.

Understandably, the manner in which the federal government funds social programs in general, and higher education in particular, will greatly affect the revenues of institutions for the near future. On a relative basis, fewer federal dollars will be directed toward higher education because of deep-rooted changes in funding philosophy and growing competition from other government sectors. In addition to the increased demands that will be felt as the baby boom generation begins to retire, other demands on the federal budget will be significant—most notably defense. Finally, many view the size of the national debt—and the increased funds needed to service it—as a serious threat to future funding.

The reexamination of the federal role in higher education raises the questions of who benefits from and who should pay for higher education. More and more policy makers believe that the balance of benefits has shifted from society as a whole to the individuals receiving the education. Many believe that the current system of higher education is overbuilt—even though many students are being turned away from public institutions because of resource limitations. A major aspect of the debate over who should pay is determining the proper balance between students and their families and the federal, state, and local governments.

Before World War II, states were largely responsible for public subsidies to public higher education in the form of low tuition. Few public funds were directed to independent institutions in the form of institutional aid. After World War II, the federal government became a more important participant in financing higher education. The G.I. Bill of Rights of 1944 provided massive sums to institutions and students. Both public and independent institutions benefited from this law and the funds it made available. The balance was altered, however, in the early 1950s when the Korean conflict G.I. Bill awarded funds for college directly to veterans rather than to the institutions. The federal government broadened its support for higher education in 1958 with the National Defense Education Act. This law provided funds to institutions as well as to students, particularly graduate students. Beginning in the late 1950s and continuing throughout much of the 1960s, the federal government provided substantial amounts of funding for facilities, equipment, libraries, research, and training. Direct aid to institutions peaked in 1965–66 and declined thereafter as federal funds shifted from institutional support to student financial aid. The 1972 Amendments to the Higher Education Act of 1965 established the policy of basing federal student assistance programs on individual student need.

Federal funds provided to higher education are divided nearly equally between student financial aid and support of research through grants and contracts, with research holding a slight edge. The latest year for which complete data are available is the federal fiscal year 2002. During that year, direct support to postsecondary education from the federal government totaled $48.5 billion. Of this amount, $25.7 billion (53 percent) supported research by colleges and universities. The remainder, $22.8 billion (47 percent) was for various student financial aid programs.[16] (These figures do not include tax credits related to the Hope Scholarship or Lifetime Learning Credits Programs. Programs like these represent indirect federal support of higher education because the amounts are provided in the form of tax deductions or credits rather than direct funding.) It is important to note that federal support for higher education does not favor either public institutions or independent institutions. The federal government has pointedly avoided favoring one sector over the other.

The philosophy guiding federal support of higher education originally was focused on enhancing access through student aid. Over time, the concept of access was broadened to include not just low-income individuals but also the middle class. For many years, higher education was viewed as the primary driver of social mobility. As a result, federal support of higher education in the form of student assistance helped achieve societal goals by providing enhanced access to education. Over time, however, circumstances have changed, and college student bodies are no longer composed exclusively, or even primarily in many cases, of 18- to 22-year-olds. More part-time students and adult learners are seeking college training while they support families and maintain jobs. For many students, the preferred option is a community college, which allows them to pursue education without sacrificing full-time employment. In addition, an increasing number of individuals are returning to college for recertification, to upgrade their professional skills, or to pursue training for an entirely new career.

For these and other budgetary reasons, the relationship between the federal government and higher education continues to evolve. As a result, the federal government is bearing less and less of the overall burden of supporting students in pursuit of advanced education. States and individual consumers of higher education (and their families) are being expected to bear more of the costs. One example is the striking shift in financial aid from grants to loans. Another is the attention given to community service as a way to be relieved of the responsibility to repay student loans.

State and Local Factors

State and local governments are the single most important source of financial support for higher education in the United States. Of the $279 billion of revenue received by all public and independent institutions during fiscal year 2000, $64.1 billion (23 percent) came from state and local government appropriations, grants, and contracts. Other major revenue sources included tuition and fees ($58.9 billion, or 21.1 percent) and federal appropriations, grants, and contracts ($25.5 billion, or 9.1 percent). The remainder comes from various sources, including auxiliary enterprises, endowment income, sales and services of educational activities, healthcare, and gifts.[17]

State and local economic and political factors have a significant impact on the financial fortunes of individual institutions. For example, the cost of energy and labor generally is lower in the Sunbelt than in the Northeast. The cost of housing typically is higher in metropolitan areas than in rural areas and becomes a factor when establishing the salary structure for faculty and staff as well as the housing rates charged to students. State and local regulations often mirror federal programs in areas such as workers' compensation, building and safety codes, public health standards, occupational health and safety programs, unemployment compensation, and retirement programs.

Several factors determine the proportion of state and local government revenues appropriated for higher education. Generally, the stronger the competition for resources in a state, the smaller the share allocated to any one social service. During the recent past, when most states have struggled financially due to the sluggish economy, higher education's priority has declined. There is nothing to suggest that higher education's status will improve in the near future. In fact, it seems likely that other programs will place greater demands on limited state resources, resulting in further cuts in higher education support. Moreover, as the federal government continues to shift the burden for various social services increasingly to the states, relatively lower-priority services such as higher education will receive smaller shares of state and local resources.

Another determinant of appropriations is the nature of the higher education structure in a state. A system composed of many community colleges is considerably less expensive to operate than one with a similar number of institutions but with more at the four-year level. Similarly, a system with multiple research institutions will have higher operating costs than one with only one research institution and several comprehensive institutions. Some states, particularly those in the Northeast, traditionally have a very strong independent sector and depend on those institutions to enroll large numbers of students who otherwise would attend public institutions. A few states, such as New Jersey, experience a considerable outmigration of potential students and allocate relatively fewer resources to higher education. Some states, such as Maryland, base their contributions to the independent sector on the level of support for public colleges and universities.

Sources of Funds

Institutions in both the public and the independent sectors rely on a variety of sources for financial support. Although the sources are similar, the relative reliance on a particular source depends on the institution's character. Independent institutions rely more heavily on student tuition and fees than do public institutions, with state appropriations making up the difference. Large research-oriented universities in both sectors receive a greater percentage of revenues from sponsors than would a comprehensive institution. Institutions with medical centers will generate significant revenues from patient care, either directly or through a physician practice plan providing support to the medical school.

Figure 2-1 presents each of the revenue types. For each type, the characteristics common to public and independent institutions are presented first; features peculiar to the sectors are presented separately. The figure does not identify student aid as a source of institutional revenue because it flows into the institution indirectly through students. (It must be noted that, for almost all sources of student aid, the institution actually receives and manages the funds. And, though the institution may recognize revenue for aid received, it reduces the amount of tuition revenue recognized in financial statements.) As noted earlier, regardless of the fact that it is only indirect revenue, federal and state support for higher education via student financial aid is considerable.

Figure 2-2 summarizes the proportions of income from the several sources of institutional revenue. There is an anomaly for one aspect of the data in the presentation. The source of these data is the Integrated Postsecondary Education Data System (IPEDS), which all degree-granting institutions must complete annually. The information presented for

FIGURE 2-1
INSTITUTIONAL RESOURCES BY SOURCE AND TYPE

Source	Type of Revenue	Received Through
Students	Tuition and fees	Customer charges
Government		
Federal	Appropriations	Subsidy
	Grants and contracts	
	–Direct costs	Exchange for services
	–Indirect costs	Reimbursement for services
State and local	Appropriations	Subsidy
	Grants and contracts	
	–Direct costs	Exchange for services
	–Indirect costs	Exchange for services
	On behalf payments	(A) Subsidy
Private		
Individuals	Gifts	Contributions
	Contributed services	(B) Subsidy
Corporate and foundations	Gifts	Contributions
	Grants and contracts	
	–Direct costs	Exchange for services
	–Indirect costs	Reimbursement for services
	Contributed services	(B) Subsidy
Institutional	Endowment income	Investment of pooled funds
	Investment income	Investment of idle balances
Sales and services	Educational activities	Customer charges
	Auxiliary enterprises	Customer charges
	Patient care	Customer charges

Notes: A–It is common for state government to pay salaries and/or fringe benefits for public colleges and universities. Such payments are recognized as both revenues and expenses.
B–Contributed services meeting specified criteria are recognized as revenues by independent institutions, but not by public institutions. The value of such services is recognized as both revenues and expenses.

Source: Adapted from 1979 Financial Responsibilities of Governing Boards.

FIGURE 2-2
SOURCES OF REVENUE FOR INSTITUTIONS OF HIGHER EDUCATION BY SECTOR AND LEVEL OF INSTITUTION, FISCAL YEAR 1999-2000

Source	Total	Public Institutions		Independent Institutions	
		Four-Year	Two-Year	Four-Year	Two-Year
		(amounts in billions)			
Government					
Federal	$25.529	$14.880	$1.522	$9.060	$0.067
State	57.493	43.693	12.676	1.099	0.025
Local	6.621	0.830	5.210	0.575	0.006
Subtotal	$89.643	$59.403	$19.408	$10.734	$0.098
Tuition and fees	58.903	23.376	5.749	29.258	0.520
Investment returns	38.944	1.147	0.023	37.698	0.076
Private sources	24.014	7.168	0.321	16.346	0.179
Auxiliary enterprises	23.521	13.596	1.578	8.261	0.086
Educational sales and services	7.689	4.596	0.221	2.838	0.034
Patient care	22.083	13.991		7.209	0.883
Other	14.231	5.716	0.994	7.365	0.156
Total	$279.028	$128.993	$28.294	$119.709	$2.032

Source	Total	Public Institutions		Independent Institutions	
		Four-Year	Two-Year	Four-Year	Two-Year
		(Percentage Distribution)			
Government					
Federal	9.1%	11.6%	5.4%	7.6%	3.3%
State	20.6%	33.9%	44.7%	0.9%	1.2%
Local	2.4%	0.6%	18.4%	0.5%	0.3%
Subtotal	32.1%	46.1%	68.5%	9.0%	4.8%
Tuition and fees	21.1%	18.1%	20.3%	24.4%	25.6%
Investment returns	14.0%	0.9%	0.1%	31.5%	3.7%
Private sources	8.6%	5.6%	1.1%	13.6%	8.8%
Auxiliary enterprises	8.4%	10.5%	5.6%	6.9%	4.2%
Educational sales and services	2.8%	3.6%	0.8%	2.4%	1.7%
Patient care	7.9%	10.8%		6.0%	43.5%
Other	5.1%	4.4%	3.6%	6.2%	7.7%
Total	100.0%	100.0%	100.0%	100.0%	100.0%

Source: National Center for Education Statistics

independent two-year institutions, though accurate, is misleading because it includes information for some hospitals that offer nursing and allied health associate degree programs. In completing the IPEDS submission, some of these hospitals included data for nonacademic revenues and classified it as patient revenue. The net effect is to increase this line item dramatically while artificially decreasing the remaining revenue categories. Rather than omit this line item and revise the percentages accordingly, the table is presented as it is provided by the National Center for Education Statistics. Readers seeking a more consistent reflection of the relative revenue sources for independent two-year institutions may wish to recast the information after excluding the patient care revenues.

Tuition and Fees

Tuition is the price of an instructional service rendered to students but, unlike most prices, it is designed to recover only a portion of the costs incurred in providing the service. Most institutions operate under the following revenue equation: cost less subsidy equals price. This model differs dramatically from the for-profit model, which uses the following equation: price less cost equals profit. Cost is only one factor taken into consideration in setting tuition levels. Other factors include:

- Tuition at peer institutions
- Other revenues—especially state appropriation for public institutions—and the need to balance the budget
- Student financial aid needs
- Tradition or philosophy of the institution (or state system)
- General economic conditions

Price setting is a very important budget decision that requires an understanding of the institution's market position and the elasticity of student demand. Demand elasticity dictates that when prices are higher, fewer students seek admission than when prices are lower. Some institutions, such as the Ivy League universities, need not be so concerned about reduced demand when they raise prices because they already turn away substantial numbers of well-qualified students. Institutions with regional audiences, on the other hand, may find that they have less flexibility when it comes to setting tuition—especially if there are comparable institutions within the same region.

To remain competitive, institutions must be sensitive to their peers' net student charges (tuition and fees less institutional student aid). Care must be taken to avoid sharing detailed information relating to specific students because it could lead to allegations of price fixing. The review of publicly available information is not a problem, however.

In comparing peer institutions, the presumed quality of education provided by each and the effect of the net price on enrollment must be considered. Tuition levels are determined by the amount of revenue needed to balance the budget within the constraints of the institutional philosophy and market position. This factor is closely related to the economic conditions in place at the time the budget is prepared. When costs increase rapidly—or when other revenues decline precipitously—tuition will rise markedly. At the same time, the institution must weigh the ability and willingness of prospective students and their families to pay higher tuition. Some institutions have strong traditions that govern the setting of tuition levels. For instance, the California public higher education system for many years had a policy of not charging tuition while maintaining low student fees. During California's economic difficulties in the early 1990s, the policy had to be abandoned as fee charges were increased markedly to provide revenues to compensate for the loss of state appropriations.

A number of independent and public institutions have attempted to provide increased support to low-income students. For instance, many independent institutions have a "need-blind" admission process in which a student's ability to pay is not considered until after the student has been admitted. Once the decision to admit has been made, the institution provides sufficient financial assistance to enable the student to attend, regardless of their financial resources. Moreover, a number of institutions have revised their methodologies for determining the amount of aid for which a student qualifies. These institutions have modified the formula used by the federal government to reduce the expected family contribution. Finally, several public institutions have revised their overall approaches to determining the amount of institutional aid that a student is eligible to receive in the form of grants so that it can be substituted for need that otherwise would be met through loans.

Some institutions seek to set tuition at a fixed percentage of the estimated annual cost of education. This policy was used in Virginia for many years until the economic downturn in the 1990s. When state appropriations failed to keep pace with the growth of institutional costs, tuition rates had to be increased to the point that the revenue exceeded the specified proportion of the annual cost of education.

Fees for special activities or purposes tend to be based as closely as possible on the actual costs of services. Examples of activities or services for which fees are charged include intercollegiate athletics, laboratory usage or breakage, instructional materials, health insurance or health services, student activities, and debt service. More recently, institutions have introduced fees that are not necessarily linked to a specific cost of service. One that has risen in popularity is a technology fee. Rarely does this fee come close to covering the full cost of providing technology services to students, but it does help provide resources that can be used to maintain or enhance those services.

Institutions with a strong commitment to student aid, such as those that provide considerable amounts of institutional aid, typically anticipate using a portion of the revenue generated through increased tuition to fund additional aid. This approach is used for two reasons. First, the institutions might risk pricing themselves out of their traditional student markets if they did not adopt this strategy. In addition, if they are committed to providing student aid to those that qualify and demonstrate a need, they will need the additional resources to sustain the commitment.

Under earlier accounting models for both public and independent institutions, student financial aid was treated as an expenditure. Tuition revenues were recognized at the amount originally assessed to the student, and the amount of financial aid used to reduce the cash payment required from the student was recognized as an expenditure. Under these circumstances, the tuition level had a significant impact on the relative revenues and expenditures related to student enrollment, but not on the institution's net revenues. With the recent changes in accounting, all aid that has been recognized as revenue at time of initial receipt is treated as a reduction of tuition revenue rather than an expenditure. Expenses for student financial aid are recognized only when a disbursement is made to the student. Although the change does not affect the institution's net cash position, it has improved the ability to manage the budgeting of tuition and student financial aid.

Independent institutions. Tuition and fees in FY 1999–2000 represented 24.4 percent of total revenues at independent four-year institutions and 25.6 percent of total revenues at independent two-year institutions.[18]

The combined value of tuition and fees typically represents a much larger percentage of revenues for independent institutions than was the case during FY 1999-2000. It is noteworthy that this was the final year of a multiyear period during which investment returns broke all previous records. (As reported in the *2000 NACUBO Endowment Study*, the average return on endowments for this year was 13 percent—significantly greater than the experience during the years since then.[19]) As a result, the percentage of revenue generated by tuition and fees actually was less than that provided by investment income.

Although investment income was substantial during this year, much of the revenue represents appreciation on investments rather than cash yield. Though beneficial in terms of an institution's overall financial position, it does not eliminate the need to charge tuition or increase tuition rates. Moreover, because tuition and fee revenues typically represent a much greater proportion of institutional revenues for the private sector than for the public sector, balancing the budget through tuition increases is a primary strategy for independent institutions.

Public institutions. Tuition and fee income in FY 1999–2000 represented 18.1 percent of total revenues at public four-year institutions and 20.3 percent of total revenues at public two-year institutions.[20] Setting tuition in the public sector often is more complicated and indirect than in the private sector. The same factors apply, but political considerations also come into play much more dramatically for public institutions. In addition, in some states, the decision is taken out of the institutions' hands because tuition pricing decisions are made either at the system level or by a state agency (or even the legislature). In states that allow institutions to establish tuition rates directly, the process is similar to what occurs in the private sector with one major exception. For some independent institutions, tuition levels are influenced significantly by available endowment income or other investment returns. In most cases, however, this influence pales in comparison with the effect of state appropriation on tuition levels for public institutions.

Depending on the state's budget process, the institution may be forced to delay setting tuition rates until the legislature has determined the appropriation and the governor has approved it. This situation proves problematic during difficult financial times, when legislatures and governors often have difficulty reaching agreement on the budget. When this happens, as it has in a few recent cases, the institution delays adjusting tuition for the fall semester and follows with a sizable increase for the second semester.

Federal Student Aid Programs

It is impossible to consider tuition and fees as a revenue source without also examining the effect of federal student financial aid. During the 1999–2000 academic year, 3.7 million full-time undergraduate students, representing 57.7 percent of all such students, received some form of federal financial aid. The comparable number for part-time undergraduate students was 3 million, representing 29.8 percent of all part-time undergraduate students.[21] The various forms of undergraduate federal financial aid are described in this section, with indications of their relative financial significance.

Pell Grants. The Higher Education Act of 1972 established the Basic Educational Opportunity Grants Program, now called the Federal Pell Grant program, to provide a minimum level of assistance that students can use at any postsecondary institution eligible to participate in Title IV programs. The funds are collected and managed by the institution and awarded to all students eligible based on the national needs analysis calculation.

The needs analysis system is scaled so that the amount of funds awarded decreases as family income increases. Actual award amounts are established based on costs of attendance at a particular institution. Total amounts available to students are limited by appropriations, and individual awards are limited by provisions that establish the maximum percentage of cost that can be covered through Pell awards. Because of the entitlement nature of the program, the maximum allowable award is revised downward by a reduction formula to ensure that sufficient funds are available in the program. The Department of Education received a $12 billion appropriation for Pell during FY 2003–04.[22] The maximum award for 2003–04 was $4,050.[23]

Campus-based programs. Unlike Pell, which is an entitlement program driven solely by needs analysis, campus-based programs are operated by the institution using funds provided by the federal government, supplemented with required matching funds. Current regulations require that institutions provide a match equal to one-third of the federal funds. Although students must demonstrate need under the same needs analysis process used for all financial aid, the programs are not entitlement programs. The institution decides which students will receive awards. The federal campus-based program funds (though administered separately) are pooled with financial aid from other sources, including the institution itself, and awarded in the form of grants, work-study, or loans.

Educational Opportunity Grants, now called Federal Supplemental Educational Opportunity Grants (FSEOG), were established by the Higher Education Act of 1965 to provide federal grants for needy students as identified by the institution. FSEOG funds are distributed to the institutions according to a state formula based on undergraduate enrollments. Supplemented by the institutional match, they are used to make grants to students. The Department of Education received a $770 million appropriation for FSEOG during FY 2003–04.[24]

The Federal Work-Study (FWS) Program was established by the Economic Opportunity Act of 1964. Funds for FWS are distributed to institutions according to a state allocation formula based on the state's proportion of higher education enrollments, high school graduates, and children in poverty-level families. Supplemented by the institutional match, they are used to pay wages to needy students employed by the institution or another nonprofit organizations. The Department of Education received an appropriation of just under $1 billion for FWS during FY 2003–04.[25]

The National Defense Student Loan Program, now called the Federal Perkins Loan Program, established by the National Defense Education Act of 1958, provides low-interest loans for needy students. Funds are distributed to institutions according to a state allocation formula based on undergraduate enrollments. The program operates as a revolving fund in that new federal funds are matched by the institution and then combined with the interest earned on previous loans and the principal repayments to make new loans. The Department of Education received an appropriation of $165 million for the Perkins Loan Program during FY 2003–04.[26] Although this seems like a relatively modest amount compared to the other programs, it must be remembered that revolving funds represent the equivalent of a perpetual fund. There are provisions for loan cancellations in return for various forms of community service, and loans occasionally are not repaid, but the interest earned on loans creates additional resources with which to make new loans.

Leveraging Educational Assistance Partnership Programs. The Higher Education Act of 1972 established the Federal-State Student Incentive Grants Program, now called the Leveraging Educational Assistance Partnership (LEAP) and the Special Leveraging Educational Assistance Partnership (SLEAP) Programs, to encourage the creation of state scholarship and community service work-study programs for needy students. The states received total appropriations of $66 million for LEAP and SLEAP during FY 2003–04.[27] Final expenditure data for FY 2003–04 are not available, but during FY 2002–03, expenditures under LEAP and SLEAP from both state and federal sources amounted to $1.2 billion.[28]

Federal Family Education Loan Program. The Higher Education Act of 1965 established the Guaranteed Student Loan Program, now called the Federal Family Education Loan (FFEL) Program. Two basic types of loans are authorized under FFEL: Stafford Loans, for undergraduate and graduate students, and Federal Parent Loans for Undergraduate Students (PLUS loans), for the parents of dependent undergraduate students. The program insures loans made by private lenders to students; reinsures loans guaranteed by state or private nonprofit agencies; subsidizes in-school interest for students up to a specified income level; and pays a special allowance to the lender to make up the difference between the student interest rate and market rates. The program is an entitlement, with annual costs to be met by the U.S. Treasury based on the dollar volume of outstanding loans, money market conditions, and the default rate.

The term FFEL now encompasses several student loan programs. In addition to Stafford Loans, the Education Amendments of 1980 established the PLUS Program as part of FFEL. The program does not subsidize in-school interest, but the federal government pays a special allowance to lenders to make up the difference between the borrower's interest rate and market rates. Full-time students may defer principal payments but not interest; part-time students must pay principal and interest in regular installments beginning 60 days after origination. The Department of Education received an appropriation of $1.9 billion for all FFEL during FY 2003–04.[29] As of FY 1999–2000, there were 6.3 million FFEL loans outstanding with a combined value of $25.7 billion.[30]

William D. Ford Federal Direct Loan Program. The newest federal loan program actually is a variant of previous programs. The Student Loan Reform Act of 1993 established the Federal Direct Student Loan Program. Under the program, the federal government is the lender and provides funds directly to student and parent borrowers through institutions. The Department of Education received an appropriation of $2.4 billion for the direct loan program during FY 2003–04.[31] As of FY 1999–2000, there were 3.1 million direct loans outstanding with a combined value of $11.8 billion.[32]

TRIO Programs. The final major category of federal financial aid is an indirect form of aid in that the funds are provided to institutions on a competitive basis for use in programs that will serve the needs of students. The funds are used to finance various programs and activities designed to assist disadvantaged students and support them in their efforts to obtain a college education. The first program, Upward Bound, grew out of the Economic Opportunity Act of 1964. The Higher Education Act of 1965 created Talent Search. The Higher Education Act of 1968 created the third program, Special Services for Disadvantaged Students, now called Student Support Services. The Department of Education received an appropriation of $833 million for the TRIO programs during FY 2003–04.[33]

State Student Aid Programs

Most states have various financial aid programs for needy students. State funds for these programs match federal money provided under the LEAP and SLEAP programs mentioned earlier. The overall amounts provided under these programs far exceed the seed funding provided by the federal government. It has become common in recent years for states to establish competitive financial aid programs. A typical scenario for these programs is for students achieving specified levels of academic performance in high school to be awarded scholarships that will continue throughout college if the students maintain a specified level of academic performance. Programs vary widely from state to state but it is not uncommon for state programs to have maximum awards, limited to tuition or an established dollar ceiling. Many states also award funds to students who attend out-of-state institutions. The total amount expended under state student aid programs during FY 2002–03 was $5.7 billion.[34]

Government Sources of Funding

Both public and independent institutions receive funding from federal, state, and local governments in the form of appropriations as well as grants and contracts. Grants are awarded on a competitive basis, and the federal government does not differentiate between public and independent institutions when making awards. Most awards include funds for direct and indirect costs. Direct costs represent the expenses incurred by the institution in undertaking the activities being supported by the grant or contract. These funds must be used exclusively for the purposes specified in the award. Typical direct costs include the salary and benefits for the principal investigator, graduate assistants, and technicians assigned to the project; supplies; travel; and any other operating expenses authorized under the award. The portion of the award related to indirect costs typically is calculated as a percentage of direct costs. The indirect costs are the institutional expenses that are not directly related to the specific project, but that provide support so that it can be conducted. Examples of indirect costs include utilities, operating expenses of various activities that support the business aspects of the project such as the accounting and payroll offices, and the cost of maintaining the space in which the project is conducted.

The federal government also provides direct appropriations to both public and independent institutions for a variety of purposes. Appropriations differ from grants and contracts in that they usually are provided through the legislative process rather than as a grant or contract. Appropriations focus on various activities and programs including libraries, cooperative education, land-grant and extension services, international education, vocational education, and a wide range of other initiatives.

Independent institutions. Revenue from federal sources, including appropriations, grants and contracts, represented 7.6 percent of the total revenues of independent four-year institutions and 3.3 percent of total revenues for independent two-year institutions during FY 1999–2000. State governments provided 0.9 percent of total revenues for independent four-year institutions and 1.2 percent for independent two-year institutions during the same period. Local governments accounted for 0.5 percent of total revenues for independent four-year institutions and 0.3 percent for independent two-year institutions during this period.[35]

State and local appropriations to independent institutions take a number of forms. A number of states contract with independent colleges and universities for a wide variety of instructional services. Many of these arrangements involve the purchase of student spaces in special programs such as health sciences. Some states support the acquisition of new facilities at independent institutions through special state grants or by allowing independent institutions to issue tax-exempt debt through state or local authorities.

A small number of states provide direct support to independent institutions in the form of contracts based on full-time equivalent enrollment of in-state students, and others appropriate funds to independent colleges and universities for capitation grants. In some cases, this can represent a substantial amount of money. For example, the 2004–05 New York appropriation bill included more than $42 million in Bundy Aid.[36] These funds are provided to "maximize the total postsecondary educational resources of New York State; promote and foster the diversity of educational options in New York State; and provide increased access to these programs by assisting institutions to minimize tuition increases."

Public institutions. Revenues from federal sources, including appropriations, grants, and contracts, represented 11.6 percent of total revenues for public four-year institutions and 5.4 percent of total revenues for public two-year institutions during FY 1999–2000. State governments provided 33.9 percent of total revenues for public four-year institutions and 44.7 percent for public two-year institutions during the same period. Local governments accounted for 0.6 percent of total revenues for public four-year institutions and 18.4 percent for public two-year institutions during this period.[37]

State and local appropriations, grants, and contracts represent the single largest source of revenue for public institutions. Nearly two-thirds of the total resources of public two-year institutions come from state and local sources. The largest percent of local resources are devoted to public two-year institutions, primarily because many community colleges are organized as part of a city or county. State and local appropriations provide resources to cover operating expenses, capital construction, and debt service.

Private Sources of Funding

Both public and independent institutions receive resources from private sources such as foundations, corporations, churches, community groups, and individuals (e.g., alumni, members of the institution's governing board, interested citizens). The resources can take many forms including gifts, grants, bequests, contributed services, and contracts for the support of research.

Many public institutions are prohibited from engaging in fund-raising activities directly. As a result, they have created foundations to pursue private support. It is typical for these foundations to both raise and manage funds in support of the public college or university. The majority of the discussion below related to independent institutions is applicable to public institutions with affiliated foundations.

There are various relationships between public institutions and their affiliated foundations. In some cases, the institution's governing board also governs the foundation. In this arrangement, the foundation operates almost as if it were a department of the institution, with all financial decisions being made by the central administration. Budgeting is relatively easy in this situation because the institution has indirect control of the foundation's resources.

There are other situations, however, in which the foundation is very independent of the institution. In this case, it is more typical for the institution to request specific support from the foundation, but not necessarily be assured of receiving it. The foundation may have established different priorities for its support. It is rare for a foundation to decline a request from the institution, but there have been some notable instances of friction between a public institution and its affiliated foundation. These situations usually can be worked out, but there have been a few instances in which the institution was forced to alter the relationship with the foundation. In a few extreme situations, the institution withdrew the right of the foundation to use the institution's name in its fund-raising activities.

Independent institutions depend more heavily than public institutions on gifts for a significant portion of each year's budget. Gifts may be designated as restricted or unrestricted and may be directed for use in the current period or be established as endowments so they can provide ongoing support through the investment income they generate. Though all gifts are valued by institutions, unrestricted gifts are the most sought after because they provide the greatest flexibility. Unrestricted gifts can be spent for any institutional purpose including current operating expenses, student aid, capital construction, payment of debt service, etc. Restricted gifts carry stipulations specifying what they can be used for and when they can be used. Despite the fact that restricted gifts do not provide as much flexibility as unrestricted gifts, they are very important to institutions. It is not uncommon for restricted gifts to be directed for purposes that the institution might otherwise undertake with its own resources. When this occurs, the institution's resources can be directed to other activities that may not be as well supported.

Although institutions depend on gift support to varying degrees in their budget strategies, these revenues are not as reliable as some other sources. In years of economic downturn, for instance, corporate giving often declines. Similarly, foundations may shift priorities away from higher education and divert their support to other social programs. Furthermore, philanthropic and corporate giving is sensitive to changes in tax laws, and events on campus can have a bearing on the level of giving by alumni and local supporters. The greater the reliance on private support, the more important it is to have contingency funding in the budget to protect against shortfalls.

Just as federal sponsored support includes resources for both direct and indirect costs, most corporate and foundation sponsors provide funds for both purposes. The major difference between governmental and private sponsors is that most private sponsors limit the rate at which indirect costs will be reimbursed. Additionally, many such sponsors limit their support to current operating expenses and will not provide support for equipment.

Some independent institutions are subsidized by religious organizations through either direct financial support or contributed services of members of the religious order. The most significant form of contributed services typically is teaching. In some institutions, the teaching members of the religious order receive salaries equal to those of lay members, and the order returns the salaries as a gift to the college or university.

Independent institutions. Revenues from private sources represented 13.6 percent of total resources for independent four-year institutions and 8.8 percent for independent two-year institutions during FY 1999–2000.[38]

Public institutions. Revenues from private sources represented 5.6 percent of total resources for public four-year institutions and 1.1 percent for public two-year institutions during FY 1999–2000.[39] It is important to note that the above percentages do not reflect the private support that was provided to affiliated foundations supporting public institutions.

Revenues from the Investment of Endowment and Other Funds

Both public and independent institutions typically have idle cash balances that can be invested to generate additional revenues. In addition to cash management programs, many institutions have sophisticated short-term investment programs. Both cash and short-term investment programs are intended to ensure that all available resources are used to generate additional revenues for the institution. (It should be noted that some public institutions are not authorized to make investments of idle cash or other resources. In these cases, the investment of the funds is managed at the state level and the state retains any investment earnings.)

Many institutions also maintain long-term investment programs. The majority of resources invested in long-term programs are in the form of endowments, which are provided by donors with a stipulation that the principal be invested in perpetuity. (For many public institutions, the endowment investments are held by an affiliated foundation but the practices discussed here are equally applicable to them.) Unlike other investment income, which usually can be used for any institutional purpose, the income generated through the investment of endowments usually is referred to as endowment income and is subject to special spending rules.

A portion of annual endowment income, which might include dividends, interest, rents, and royalties, is made available for the purpose designated by the donor or, if no purpose was specified, for the general purposes of the institution. The amount available in a given year is determined by the application of a formula, referred to as the spending or payout rate. This rate usually is calculated based on the historical market value of the endowment and may also take into consideration the amount made available in the prior year.

If investment income generated by the endowment in a given year is insufficient to meet the spending level authorized under the payout calculation, the income is supplemented from accumulated gains and/or market appreciation. These amounts accumulate when the combined value of gains, market appreciation, and investment income exceeds the amount determined under the spending rate calculation. When this occurs, the funds are reinvested in the endowment as a hedge against downturns in the economy.

Endowment size varies dramatically from sector to sector and institution to institution. The largest higher education endowment is held by Harvard University. During FY 2003–04, Harvard's endowment grew to $22.6 billion.[40] The largest endowment held by a public institution is that of the University of Texas System, which grew to $10.3 billion during FY 2003-04.[41] Although these amounts are very impressive, they are not representative of higher education. Of the approximately 700 institutions participating in the *2003 NACUBO Endowment Study*, less than 300 have endowments exceeding $100 million, and less than 90 of these have endowments exceeding $500 million.[42] Thus, for the vast majority of institutions, endowment income is quite small.

Independent institutions. Revenues from the investment of endowment and other financial assets represented 31.5 percent of total revenues at independent four-year institutions and 3.7 percent of total revenues at independent two-year institutions during FY 1999–2000.[43]

Public institutions. Revenues from the investment of endowment and other financial assets represented 0.9 percent of total revenues at public four-year institutions and 0.1 percent of total revenues at public two-year institutions during FY 1999–2000.[44] If the investment revenue from affiliated foundations was included in the amounts, the percentages would be higher, but significantly less than that of independent institutions.

Income from Sales and Services and Other Sources

Colleges and universities receive revenue from the sale of educational and patient care services as well as from auxiliary enterprises. Educational activities might include laboratory and other testing services, demonstration schools, dairy creameries, hotels, college theaters, and numerous other academic activities that, through instruction, create goods or services which can be sold to the general public. Patient care services are provided through teaching hospitals, outpatient clinics, student and staff health and counseling centers, and hearing and speech clinics. Auxiliary enterprises, which typically are self-supporting, include activities such as residence and dining halls, bookstores, student unions, parking and transit operations, and—in the case of some institutions—intercollegiate athletics.

Both public and independent institutions have a wide range of miscellaneous revenue sources that, individually, do not represent major sources of revenue. Rather than attempt to capture specific data about these sources, IPEDS includes a category for revenues that do not fit in the primary sources already discussed. Though individually relatively insignificant, collectively they represent a substantial amount of revenue. These items could include gains on the sale of surplus property such as obsolete or unneeded equipment, insurance recoveries resulting from natural disasters or other property damage, or other miscellaneous activities that are not part of the primary academic mission.

Independent institutions. Revenues from sales and services represented 9.3 percent of total revenues at independent four-year institutions and 5.9 percent of total revenues at independent two-year institutions during FY 1999–2000. The comparable amounts for other revenues were 6.2 percent and 7.7 percent, respectively.[45]

Public institutions. Revenues from sales and services represented 14.1 percent of total revenues at public four-year institutions and 6.4 percent of total revenues at public two-year institutions during FY 1999–2000. The comparable amounts for other revenues were 4.4 percent and 3.6 percent, respectively.[46]

Notes

[1]James Harvey et al., *Straight Talk about College Costs and Prices: The Report of the National Commission on the Cost of Higher Education* (Washington, DC: American Institutes for Research, 1998).

[2] Ibid.

[3] Eric Hoover, "Public Colleges See a 10% Rise in Tuition for 2004–5," *The Chronicle of Higher Education,* October 29, 2004.

[4] National Center for Education Statistics, "Degree-granting Institutions, by Control and Type of Institution: 1949-50 to 2002-03," http://nces.ed.gov/programs/digest/d03/tables/dt246.asp (accessed August 5, 2004).

[5] EDUCAUSE, *The Pocket Guide to U.S. Higher Education*, (Boulder, Colorado: EDUCAUSE, 2003).

[6] National Center for Education Statistics, "Total Fall Enrollment in Degree-granting Institutions, by Attendance Status, Sex of Student, and Control of Institution: 1947 to 2001," http://nces.ed.gov/programs/digest/d03/tables/dt174.asp (accessed August 5, 2004).

[7] National Center for Education Statistics, "Employees in Degree-granting Institutions of Higher Education, by Primary Occupation, Employment Status, and Control of Institution: Fall 1976, Fall 1991, and Fall 2001," http://nces/ed/gov/programs/digest/d03/tables/dt226.asp (accessed August 5, 2004).

[8] Editors of *The Chronicle of Higher Education, The Almanac of Higher Education 1994* (Chicago: University of Chicago Press, 1994).

[9] Harvey H. Kaiser and Jerry S. Davis, *A Foundation to Uphold: A Study of Facilities Conditions at U.S. Colleges and Universities* (Alexandria, Virginia: APPA: The Association of Higher Education Facilities Officers, 1996).

[10] Susanna Tulley, "IT by the Numbers," *The Chronicle of Higher Education*, January 30, 2004.

[11] Ibid.

[12] Paul E. Lingenfelter et al. *State Higher Education Finance FY 2003* (Denver, Colorado: State Higher Education Executive Officers, 2004).

[13] Ibid.

[14] National Center for Education Statistics, "Projections of Education Statistics to 2013," http://nces.ed.gov/programs/projections/ch 2.asp (accessed August 5, 2004).

[15] Western Interstate Commission for Higher Education, *Knocking at the College Door* (Boulder, Colorado: Western Interstate Commission for Higher Education, 2003).

[16] National Center for Education Statistics, "Federal Education Support and Estimated Federal Tax Expenditures for Education, by Category: Fiscal Tears 1965 to 2002,"http://nces.gov/programs/digest/d02/dt363.asp (accessed August 6, 2004).

[17] National Center for Education Statistics, "Current-fund Revenue of Public Degree-granting Institutions, by Source of Funds and by Type of Institution: 1999–2000" and "Total Revenue of Private Not-for-profit Degree-granting Institutions, by Source of Funds and by Type of Institution: 1999-2000," http://nces.ed.gov/programs/digest/d02/dt334.asp and http://nces.ed.gov/programs/digest/d02/dt335.asp (accessed August 2, 2004).

[18] Ibid.

[19] National Association of College and University Business Officers, *2000 NACUBO Endowment Study*, (Washington, DC: National Association of College and University Business Officers, 2001).

[20] National Center for Education Statistics, "Current-fund Revenue of Public Degree-granting Institutions, by Source of Funds and by Type of Institution: 1999-2000" and "Total Revenue of Private Not-for-profit Degree-granting Institutions, by Source of Funds and by Type of Institution: 1999-2000," http://nces.ed.gov/programs/digest/d02/dt334.asp and http://nces.ed.gov/programs/digest/d02/dt335.asp (accessed August 2, 2004).

[21] National Center for Education Statistics, "Undergraduates Enrolled Full-time and Part-time, by Federal Aid Program and by Control and Level of Institution: 1999-2000,"http://nces.ed.gov/programs/digest/d02/dt322.asp (accessed August 6, 2004).

[22] Department of Education, "Budget History," http://nces.ed.gov/about/overview/budget/history/edhistory.xls (accessed August 6, 2004).

[23] Department of Education, "Federal Pell Grants," http://studentaid.ed.gov/students/publications/FYE/2004 2005/english/federalpell-grants.htm#top (accessed August 6, 2004).

[24] Department of Education, "Budget History," http://www.ed.gov/about/overview/budget/history/edhistory.xls (accessed August 6, 2004).

[25] Ibid.

[26] Ibid.

[27] Greg Gerrans, "LEAP and SLEAP Update," presentation at National Association of State Student Grant and Aid Programs Spring Conference, Washington, DC, May 25, 2004, http://www.fp.ed.gov/fp/attachments/activities_whatsnew/NASSG APSPRING04final.ppt#256,1, (accessed August 6, 2004).

[28] Ibid.

[29] Department of Education, "Budget History," http://www.ed.gov/about/overview/budget/history/edhistory.xls (accessed August 6, 2004).

[30] National Center for Education Statistics, "Undergraduates Enrolled Full-time and Part-time, by Federal Aid Program and by Control and Level of Institution: 1999–2000," http://nces.ed.gov/programs/digest/d02/dt322.asp (accessed August 6, 2004).

[31] Department of Education, "Budget History," http://www.ed.gov/about/overview/budget/history/edhistory.xls (accessed August 6, 2004).

[32] National Center for Education Statistics, "Undergraduates Enrolled Full-time and Part-time, by Federal Aid Program and by Control and Level of Institution: 1999–2000," http://nces.ed.gov/programs/digest/d02/dt322.asp (accessed August 6, 2004).

[33] Department of Education, "Budget History," http://www.ed.gov/about/overview/budget/history/edhistory.xls (accessed August 6, 2004).

[34] Greg Gerrans, "LEAP and SLEAP Update," op. cit.

[35] National Center for Education Statistics, "Current-fund Revenue of Public Degree-granting Institutions, by Source of Funds and by Type of Institution: 1999–2000" and "Total Revenue of Private Not-for-profit Degree-granting Institutions, by Source of Funds and by Type of Institution: 1999–2000," http://nces.ed.gov/programs/digest/d02/dt334.asp and http://nces.ed.gov/programs/digest/d02/dt335.asp (accessed August 2, 2004).

[36] State of New York Education, Labor and Family Assistance Budget, http://publications.budget.state.ny.us/fy0405approbills/elfa.pdf, page 56.

[37] National Center for Education Statistics, "Current-fund Revenue of Public Degree-granting Institutions, by Source of Funds and by Type of Institution: 1999–2000" and "Total Revenue of Private Not-for-profit Degree-granting Institutions, by Source of Funds and by Type of Institution: 1999–2000," http://nces.ed.gov/programs/digest/d02/dt334.asp and http://nces.ed.gov/programs/digest/d02/dt335.asp (accessed August 2, 2004).

[38] Ibid.

[39] Ibid.

[40] Chronicle of Higher Education, September 24, 2004, Money & Management section.

[41] Debbie Frederick, email message to author, November 2, 2004.

[42] National Association of College and University Business Officers, *2003 NACUBO Endowment Study* (Washington, DC: National Association of College and University Business Officers, 2004).

[43] National Center for Education Statistics, "Current-fund Revenue of Public Degree-granting Institutions, by Source of Funds and by Type of Institution: 1999–2000" and "Total Revenue of Private Not-for-profit Degree-granting Institutions, by Source of Funds and by Type of Institution: 1999–2000," http://nces.ed.gov/programs/digest/d02/dt334.asp and http://nces.ed.gov/programs/digest/d02/dt335.asp (accessed August 2, 2004).

[44] Ibid.

[45] Ibid.

[46] Ibid.

chapter three

THE BUDGET PROCESS

Despite the differing characteristics and financial models of public and independent institutions, the reality is that they tend to follow essentially the same general budget process. The key variant, applicable to some public institutions, is the impact the state's budget process may have on the timing of specific aspects of the institution's process. At a global level, however, the same steps must be taken by the same individuals in the same sequence over roughly the same time frame. The particular organizational structure of an institution may dictate that a particular office will take certain steps, but in most instances, the basic steps will occur regardless of the type of institution.

The general process applies across the board, but institutional characteristics dictate some differences. For instance, institutional size has a significant impact. The larger the institution, the more likely it is that the budget process includes more participants and is decentralized, at least to some degree. Smaller institutions may rely exclusively on a centralized approach using top-down directives covering budget matters. Mission comes into play as well. Institutions with a major research mission and significant amounts of external funding will use different approaches than an institution that depends primarily on tuition for its revenue.

Less tangible factors also come into play. For instance, the relative trust among campus groups influences the nature of the process. The greater the trust among the administration, faculty, and other stakeholder groups, the more likely the campus will be to employ an open process with significant information sharing. In organizations that lack trust, the budget process will more likely involve only a small group of individuals and result in a final product that is not necessarily well understood outside this group. It should be noted that this type of closed process ultimately will erode whatever trust might exist. In fact, when trust is a problem on a campus, the budget process sometimes is a significant part of the problem.

A key consideration in the budget process is the timing of various activities. The term used to describe the timetable is the budget cycle. At any time, a campus will be in some phase of both an operating budget and a capital budget. The operating budget cycle for a given fiscal year runs from the initial research and analysis undertaken to support the establishment of budget assumptions all the way through the retroactive analysis used to assess how well the actual results compare with what had been projected. Many believe that the budget cycle isn't completed until the financial statement audit has been concluded. At that point, the budgeted results are finalized. Depending on the institution, the overall budget cycle can last up to 24 months. For public institutions, the cycle can be even longer.

Due to the types of projects included in a capital budget, its cycle will be much longer. Several years may elapse from the time a project is conceptualized to the point when it is removed from the budget because it has been completed and placed in service. Because multiple projects may be in different phases at any point, capital budgets tend to stretch out for six or more years.

Roles

In an optimal environment, individuals throughout the campus participate in the budget process in a variety of ways. They serve on committees that develop the plans for the institution; they are involved in analyzing the information used to establish the assumptions that guide budget development; and they develop the rationales to support the continued investment of resources in the mission-critical activities of the institution. The sad reality is that few institutions have an inclusive planning and budgeting process, so most individuals on campus do not influence the plans or the budgets intended to implement them.

Without meaningful opportunities for participation in the planning and budgeting process, two overarching roles evolve: spender and cutter. The spender, or advocacy, role is focused on obtaining the maximum allocation of resources for the spender's unit or activity. The cutter, or restraining, role focuses on conserving resources, either for new initiatives or to increase reserves.

A typical spender role is that of a department chairperson. It is his or her responsibility to protect the resources made available in the current budget. If this is not accomplished, the chairperson will have failed in one of the primary responsibilities of the position—being an advocate for the unit. Remember that no unit believes it has sufficient resources to do everything it feels it could—or achieve the quality levels to which it aspires. Therefore, if the chairperson can't at least protect the level of resources currently being received, the faculty has a negative response. On the other hand, a chairperson who is able to garner increased resources—especially as compared with peer departments—can fall short in other areas and still be well regarded by the department's faculty. The added resources may be used for new programs, improved staffing, substantial salary increases, and other purposes. In some ways, it doesn't really matter how the resources are allocated—just that they have been obtained.

The role of the cutter can be performed at various levels of the institution. For instance, the dean may be seeking ways to cut resources from one unit in order to provide resources needed by another unit—or to undertake a new college-level initiative. Although the dean clearly is an advocate for the unit, from the perspective of the department facing a reduction in resources, the dean is functioning in the same manner as the budget office—the traditional cutter.

On most campuses, the budget office is perceived to be the ultimate cutter. This unit is charged with development of the overall budget. The expectation is a budget that reflects the priorities established for the institution, one that is fiscally responsible, and one that has sufficient flexibility to respond to unanticipated circumstances. To accomplish the objective, the budget office likely will be forced to reject requests for additional funds from some academic and administrative units while providing increased funds to others—for example, to cover uncontrollable cost increases such as utilities or to fund new faculty for a recently authorized graduate program. Despite the perception, however, the budget office staff usually isn't the cutter. Most often, the budget office is merely applying the effect of the decisions made either through the planning process or as part of the budget assumptions approved by the board. Rarely is a budget office in the position of actually making budget allocation decisions.

Factors Affecting the Budget Process

Various factors influence the budget process. Some are ingrained in the institution's character. Others result from the strong personalities of individuals in influential positions. Still others are a function of the institution's governance model. Understanding these factors will go a long way toward determining how to influence the budget.

Institutional Character

The most important factor influencing the budget process is institutional character. There are nearly 4,000 public and independent higher education institutions, each with a unique character shaped by its culture, operating climate, administrative structure, and history. Size and mission are factors that contribute to institutional character, as does status as a public or independent institution. Moreover, not all independent institutions are created or operated equally. Religiously affiliated institutions have a very different character from that of other independent institutions.

Similarly, public land-grant universities are unlike public regional comprehensive universities. Flagship institutions have a different character from that of small regional public colleges, especially if the latter is an "open-admission" institution with a low retention rate. For the most part, all public institutions are resource-constrained, and this reality affects their institutional character. Flagship institutions, however, are much more likely to enjoy strong political support in the state legislature, an asset that influences institutional character as well as the institution's constituencies.

The character of a community college is different from that of a four-year institution and, among community colleges, there are additional variations. Most community colleges are located in urban settings—whether inner city or suburban. Others, however, are located in rural settings, primarily to provide access to all citizens in a state.

The character of the student attracted to the institution will have a bearing on institutional character. For instance, students attending an inner-city campus are more likely to have remedial needs that may not be as common for a community college in a suburban setting. Similarly, the presence or absence of vocational partnerships with local industry will influence the character of the institution, as will the level of coordination with local K–12 educational systems.

Each dimension of an institution's character contributes to the way in which participants in the budgetary process interact. What works well in one environment may not translate well to another environment. Simpler logistics may permit smaller colleges and universities to allow more participation by faculty and students in the budget process. Smaller institutions can involve a relatively small number of participants and still have representation from all segments of the institution. This approach is much more difficult for a large institution, which might allow the same number of participants but not have the same level of representation.

Participants in the budget process at public institutions and at elite independent institutions will establish different patterns for the budget process and ask different questions about resource allocation than those at struggling institutions. Because of their reliance on public funding, public institutions are accountable to a broader constituency than private institutions. They must be responsive to legislators, state agencies, and the public in ways that independent institutions are not. Even in states where higher education enjoys significant levels of autonomy, there still are requirements to provide information to state agencies. These demands may shape the formats for budget requests, accounting structures, and other aspects of regulatory oversight. Both public and private institutions are subject to extensive accountability requirements for resources provided by the federal government—whether directly to the institution in the form of research grants or to students, through the institution, in the form of financial aid.

Regardless of the budget strategy employed at an institution, it is highly likely that those responsible for administering the process will pay close attention to what is happening at other institutions. One of the unique characteristics of higher education is the relative ease with which best practices are shared among institutions. Although colleges and universities complete for sponsored program funding, for the most qualified students, and on athletic fields, campuses are more than willing to share new ideas and successes with their peers. Entire conferences are devoted to the sharing of success stories, best practices, and innovative approaches to a variety of management issues.

In this regard, budgeting is no exception and the character of the institution will influence how readily a new strategy can be implemented. Typically, though, change is introduced incrementally. Few institutions have a culture that can tolerate a completely new approach to something as crucial as budgeting. As a result, it's common for institutions to retain the basic elements of existing budget strategies while introducing new approaches through pilot programs or for only a portion of the overall budget.

The nature of campus decision making has implications for the budget process as well. A college or university with a well-developed decentralized academic administration and significant faculty participation will react negatively if major budget decisions are made in a top-down manner with no opportunity for faculty involvement. On the other hand, the faculty at a community college with only limited decentralized academic administration and a heavy reliance on adjunct faculty may be very comfortable leaving the budget decisions to administrators who work with these matters every day.

Involvement

Individual campuses exhibit differing levels of involvement by various stakeholder groups on campus. The level of involvement for faculty and students, in particular, has a significant influence on their satisfaction with the decisions that shape the resource allocations. Faculty play a critical role with respect to academic program development, including new instructional endeavors, research institutes, and service programs. They often believe that they have unique perspectives that should be considered.

Students are not necessarily as active on campus as faculty—especially compared with earlier generations—but they still seek to influence budget decisions. As prices have risen and the federal government has increased the use of loans in lieu of grants, students are paying closer attention to decisions that affect the price of an education. Even in situations in which students do not have a formal voice with respect to budget matters, their views become apparent through their enrollment decisions. If students elect not to enroll in certain programs, the institution eventually will have to reduce resources allocated to those programs.

As budget processes evolve over time, involvement by various constituencies also changes. For those seeking to influence the amount of resources allocated to a particular activity, involvement at the budget stage usually is less effective than involvement in planning decisions. If an institution plans effectively, budgetary decisions naturally evolve from the planning process. By the time the budget process is under way, the critical decisions already have been made. Nevertheless, because relatively few institutions do an effective job of linking planning with budgeting, interested parties always should seek to participate at the budget stage.

They must recognize, however, that even when their involvement is solicited, not all ideas or opinions are weighed equally. Some requests are simply pleas for more, with no evidence to demonstrate the benefits that will come from the additional allocation. In other situations, strong cases are made with ample evidence of what can be accomplished with increased resources. Even if the case is valid, the allocations may not be made if the outcomes are not consistent with the priorities established for the budget process.

Everyone must understand that the development of a budget is an arduous, time-consuming process. Those who want to participate in the process must be prepared to invest the time and effort to become familiar with the issues and the competing priorities for resources. For that reason, excessive turnover within constituent groups seeking to influence budget decisions will be counterproductive. Individuals given the opportunity to participate must commit significant effort for several years to learn enough to offer meaningful input. Unfortunately, the budget process will take participants away from their primary reasons for being part of the academy—teaching or research in the case of faculty, or studying in the case of students. Faculty, of course, will be credited with service, but the benefit to students is less tangible.

Different governance structures require different levels of involvement. Moreover, the involvement can occur at varying stages. A shared governance model may require a high level of faculty, staff, and student participation. These groups typically will be involved at the planning stage, as budget assumptions are being developed and approved, and throughout the budget process itself. Individuals representing various constituencies have significant involvement, and their views are reflected in the final budget that is submitted to the board for approval. It's interesting to note that when meaningful involvement is allowed and even encouraged, constituents frequently find it easier to adopt an institutional perspective. Rather than merely advocate for the results that would be most advantageous for their own constituency, these individuals recognize the global needs of the institution and support what's best for the greatest number.

A slightly less participatory model may provide opportunities for faculty and/or student involvement through an advisory committee. In this model, a widely representative committee is established at the outset of the budget process. The committee has an opportunity to be involved in various components of the budget process, and their input typically is sought throughout. Unlike the shared governance model, advisory committees frequently discover that they do not have much impact. Sometimes the committee's contributions are sought on relatively few issues or issues that are not particularly significant. In this situation, the individuals often identify themselves as advocates for their constituencies, making it difficult for the committee to reach a consensus that can be considered by those making final decisions on budget allocations.

Some colleges and universities structure formal participation in the budget process to occur at key points during the budget cycle. Faculty, student, and administrative budget committees may be involved in major budget decision making. The most practical role for faculty and students is to help establish program and activity priorities and to recommend general support levels. Faculty participation is appropriate and especially useful in evaluating proposals from deans or program heads for the allocation of faculty positions.

Although budget development can be a highly participatory process involving all segments of a campus, budget implementation and monitoring responsibilities usually are carried out by two specific units: the central accounting office (sometimes referred to as the controller's office) and the budget office. In addition to other duties, the central accounting office must monitor and report on the progress of the institution toward (1) actually receiving the projected revenues and (2) expending the resources allocated to the various units. Although those with primary responsibility for administering specific accounts are the ones who carry out the day-to-day activities that produce revenues or expend resources, they are involved with only a small part of the overall financial picture. The central accounting office assembles all of the parts to create the high-level picture indicating whether the institution is on track to meet its budget targets while it pursues its many activities.

While the central accounting office is monitoring and reporting on the global activity of the college or university, the budget office is engaged in at least two specific activities: reviewing requests for changes to the current approved budget and preparing for the next budget cycle. Personnel activities such as unexpected retirements, resignations, or extended illnesses will necessitate changes in the way salaries and benefits are deployed. When a key faculty member is seriously ill, for example, the department may request supplemental funding to pay overload to others in the department or to engage adjunct faculty to cover the faculty member's class sections. Or a principal investigator may learn of a new grant opportunity that she is assured of receiving if the institution can commit matching funds. There is no end to the budget issues that arise each day on a campus. The budget office staff are the ones who must react to these issues and make recommendations in accordance with the established structure for addressing them.

While addressing individual budget issues on a day-to-day basis, the budget staff are also considering the future implications of the issues. In some cases, these situations are temporary and will resolve themselves by the end of the year. In other cases, however, the ongoing implications must be addressed. For instance, if a faculty member's research grant is a multiyear award, the demand for matching funds will continue beyond the current period. If the review process results in approval of the matching funds, this ongoing commitment must be factored into future-year budgets.

Other matters that would affect future-year budgets include analysis of the results of the tenure process, changes in the endowment payout authorized for the future, decisions related to program expansion or contraction, and the impact of new construction. Others will make final decisions regarding these matters, but the budget office staff must consider the impact on the core budget for the future.

Openness of the Process

The degree to which the budget process is open to casual review by those not actively involved in the deliberations dictates the amount of flexibility decision makers have in their negotiations over resource allocations. The openness of the process, in turn, is determined by the institution's character and structure for involvement. The greater the number of participants in the process, the more open it will be.

At some institutions the degree of openness is carefully controlled to prevent unintended consequences. For instance, if the budget provides for changes that might result from outsourcing a part of physical plant operations, great care must be taken in how these changes are communicated. Outsourcing analysis usually includes significant attention to the outsource candidate's plans with respect to existing employees. Nevertheless, when staff learn about such a possibility through the budget process, they are likely to be alarmed by the news, resulting in significant service disruptions until the matter can be addressed.

As a rule, budgets should not contain surprises for the campus community. Important issues should be addressed before they affect the budget—ideally, through an engaged and inclusive planning process. If difficult issues do arise at the budget development stage, it is advisable to separate them from budgetary implications, consider them with care, and, if appropriate, communicate the decision to affected parties. Then the budgetary implications can be addressed. This approach doesn't necessarily prevent acrimony or concerns, but it will help forestall challenges to the budget as a whole. If the budget contains major surprises—especially ones that could have been addressed in a more open manner—the entire process becomes suspect.

In the recent past, the policy-making and decision-making arenas have become more open, especially at public institutions that are subject to "open meetings" legislation and/or regulations. Many view this development as a positive one because it enhances the accountability of those in public positions. It can have negative consequences, however. By its nature, budget development is a process of negotiation and tradeoff. Even when conducted in an above-board and appropriate manner, it can be viewed in a negative light. Some have compared budget development to making sausage. Although the result may be appealing, the process of getting there includes some undesirable elements. The negotiation process will likely result in the identification of some institutional activities that can be sacrificed in favor of others that will provide substantial long-term benefits. Voicing this fact publicly can be difficult—especially for those who are representing a particular constituency that will be affected adversely through the negotiation.

Recognizing the need for a balance between openness and privacy, some institutions have designed the budget process to allow the interests of relevant groups to be represented while sensitive discussions about competing priorities are conducted. Accordingly, communications to the broader academic community are structured to minimize the negative impact that budget decisions may have on individuals, programs, and activities. In these circumstances, the need for openness in the budget process is balanced against the need for privacy during delicate negotiations and deliberations.

Decision-Making Authority

A continual source of tension among decision makers in any organizational setting—but especially when dealing with resource allocation—is determining the level of authority at which decisions should be made. Most individuals feel that those above them should give them greater autonomy. Department chairpersons feel constrained by deans, deans feel constrained by the provost, and—in public institutions—everyone complains about approvals required by the legislative or executive branch.

At what level should financial decisions be made? Most experts believe that the best decisions are those that are made closest to the action. In fact, the real issue is where the organization is on the continuum between control and accountability. A system of accountability allows greater latitude with respect to decision making than one that relies on controls to prevent problems from occurring.

Controls can be an element of an accountability system, but they need not be the dominant factor. It might be appropriate to allow a system of accountability to operate for most transactions and decisions, with control being exercised only for selected issues that represent significant dollar risk. For instance, a higher authority typically is required to approve transactions above a certain dollar level or to sign off when an official salary offer is made to a prospective employee. This level of control is appropriate to ensure that proper procedures have been followed and that the financial commitment fits within the overall needs of the institution.

It is critical to maintain an appropriate balance between the level of control and the amount of latitude provided to operational managers. Clearly there is a need to avoid mistakes with large dollar implications, but this need must be weighed against the inefficiencies of a process that requires numerous approvals for relatively small-dollar purchases. The specific point will vary from institution to institution, and it should be examined periodically to ensure that the controls are not being applied at too low a level.

Decisions about the allocation of scarce resources typically are made at the highest levels. As resources become scarcer, it is even more critical to assure that resources are deployed in the most effective manner. Coupled with these concerns is the demand for increased accountability. With resource allocations being made at higher levels, the requests for documentation and justification are increasing, primarily because those at the higher levels have less direct knowledge of organization-wide activities. This combination of factors requires that institutional leaders guard against setting decision-making authority at too high a level so that it eliminates the flexibility to address issues as they arise.

Operating Budget Cycle

At any time, multiple budgets are being used, developed, or analyzed on a retrospective basis. For this reason, multiple budget cycles also are transpiring. The discussion in this section focuses on the operating budget, but readers should recognize that operating budgets are closely integrated with capital budgets. Operating budgets address revenues and reserves, both of which may be sources for some projects addressed in the capital budget. Similarly, the facilities projects covered by a capital budget will affect the operating budget once they are completed and placed in service. The expenses for maintaining the facilities become part of operating expenses, and, if the facilities are debt-financed, the interest on the long-term debt will be a claim on resources. Clearly, operating and capital budgets cannot be developed in isolation.

The operating budget cycles for Northwestern University and the University of Virginia are similar in many ways (see Figures 3-1 and 3-2), but because the University of Virginia is a public institution, its process has additional steps linked to state submissions. The nature of the state budgeting cycle requires campuses and other state agencies to meet various deadlines and, in most cases, to submit information on a somewhat piecemeal basis. This cycle can be contrasted with Northwestern University's process, which appears to flow in a more natural sequence. Despite the differences, the basic tasks must occur on both campuses. Although smaller, less complex institutions may require a more streamlined budget process, the general flow presented in Figures 3–1 and 3–2 could be adapted to any public or independent institution.

FIGURE 3-1

OPERATING BUDGET DEVELOPMENT CYCLE
FOR THE UNIVERSITY OF VIRGINIA

June 30   Prior fiscal year ends.

September   *In odd-number years, submit base operating budget and activity-based budget for the upcoming biennium to the state.*

September–
October   Present operating and capital budget requests (odd-number years) or amendments (even-number years) to governing board for approval.

October   *Submit biennial budget request. In even-number years, the request represents amendment to existing biennial budget; in odd-number years, the request is for the upcoming biennium.*

December   *Governor submits budget to the General Assembly.*

Distribute upcoming fiscal year budget development instructions and templates to vice presidents for distribution to reporting units (after applying any unit-specific revisions).

Process all modifications that will affect target budgets for the upcoming fiscal year.

Tuition, housing, and board fee increase requests for upcoming fiscal year due for designated programs.

January   *Submit budget amendments to the General Assembly for items not addressed by the governor's proposed budget.*

Distribute internal budget targets to the vice presidents for distribution to reporting units (after applying any unit-specific adjustments).

Application, activity, and other fee increase requests for upcoming fiscal year due.

Begin development of tuition proposal and financial aid allocations.

February   *Cross-over of state budget bills from house and senate.*

Mandatory fee increase requests for upcoming fiscal year due.

Full budget submissions due from auxiliary enterprises, selected other self-supporting units, and various academic units.

General ledger budget detail for upcoming fiscal year must be entered into Integrated System for Academic Division.

Present upcoming fiscal year housing rates and budget development assumptions to the governing board for approval.

March   *Joint conference committee forwards General Assembly-approved budget bill to governor.*

Budget submission for upcoming fiscal year due from UVa College at Wise.

April   All remaining budget submissions, including addenda requests, for upcoming fiscal year due for Academic Division.

Budget submission for upcoming fiscal year due from Medical Center.

Present dining, tuition, and mandatory fee proposal to governing board for approval.

May   *Appropriation act approved by General Assembly and governor.*

Carryforward requests for current fiscal year budget due.

Present budget to governing board for approval.

Distribute approved budget and addenda to vice presidents.

July 1   New fiscal year begins.

Implement new state budget.

Implement new university budget.

Items in italics represent submissions to the state or activities that occur at the state level.

Source: University of Virginia Budget Office

FIGURE 3-2

OPERATING BUDGET DEVELOPMENT CYCLE FOR NORTHWESTERN UNIVERSITY

August 31   Prior fiscal year ends.

September   Units review current fiscal year budgets to verify accuracy.

October–
December   Administrative Planning & Budget Group meets to:
- Review and discuss budget planning strategies/procedures.
- Review and discuss program priorities.
- Review and discuss preliminary revenue planning assumptions.
- Set planning parameters for upcoming fiscal year.

November–
March   Central administration staff (including Budget Office, Provost's Office, and Administration & Planning) meet with deans and other unit heads to review and update strategic plans (pre-planning meetings).

University Administration meets with deans and other unit heads to discuss strategic plans (planning and budget meetings).

December   Trustee Budget Committee meets to review final budget performance results for prior fiscal year and the planning schedule for the upcoming fiscal year's budget development process.

February   Preliminary allocation materials distributed.

Trustee Budget Committee reviews preliminary budget performance report for current fiscal year and receives status report on upcoming fiscal year budget planning.

Trustees review and approve tuition and room & board rates for upcoming fiscal year.

March   Faculty salary planning guidelines distributed to schools.

April   Upcoming fiscal year budget allocations are finalized.

Budget Office prepares and distributes final budget allocation materials and detailed budget preparation materials for upcoming fiscal year.

Administrative Retreat.

May   Faculty salary plans due to Provost's Office.

Detailed upcoming fiscal year appropriated budgets due to Budget Office.

Faculty hiring plans for all schools due to Provost's Office.

Budget Office reviews upcoming fiscal year appropriated budget detail and reconciles with final budget summary.

Budget Office prepares budget summary for upcoming fiscal year for review by the President and Trustees.

Exempt and non-exempt staff salary plans due to Human Resources.

June   Trustee Budget Committee reviews and endorses final upcoming fiscal year operating budget and receives status report on current fiscal year budget performance.

July   Upcoming fiscal year budget detail entered into financial system.

August   Upcoming fiscal year budgets are distributed to units.

September 1   New fiscal year begins.

Source: Northwestern University Budget Planning and Allocation Calendar

Budgeting is an iterative process at both public and independent institutions. Although the approach may appear straightforward and sequential, it is more likely that many steps will be revisited between the starting point and the board's final approval. For example, it is common for some submissions to be returned at different steps because they are not consistent with the established guidelines or they simply represent unrealistic proposals. Even with this "back-and-forth" method, the following are typical steps in a budget process, listed in the order in which they usually occur:

- Close out the prior fiscal year.

- Analyze year-to-date results for the current year along with the final results for the prior year.

- Develop the plans to support the budget.

- Project enrollment and related demographic changes evolving from plans.

- Establish budget assumptions for the board's approval.

- Develop projections of central revenues.

- Develop projections of expense factors.

- Develop and distribute guidelines for preparing budget proposals.

- Develop and submit budget proposals up through the organizational chain.

- Analyze submissions, assuring their compliance with guidelines, and prepare a comprehensive operating budget.

- Obtain board approval of the budget.

- Begin budget implementation.

Prior-year closeout. Budgets always are being developed in the midst of one fiscal year, and a key input is information from the latest year for which final results are available. Prior-year closeout is the process of finalizing all revenue and expense activity in preparation for the annual financial statement audit.

Various actions must occur as part of the closeout process, which begins well in advance of fiscal year-end. The overall objective is to ensure sufficient time for the orderly conduct of financial activity. For public institutions that may face the reversion of unexpended funds, a critical step is assuring that funds are spent wisely for legitimate purposes rather than being returned to the state.

Because last-minute spending may result in the acquisition of goods that may not be needed, it's not uncommon for some institutions to implement supplemental review processes for transactions above a certain dollar amount that are initiated close to year-end. Similarly, it's common for campuses to specify that some types of purchases—particularly equipment—cannot be initiated after a certain date. These procedures stem not only from concerns about workload for procurement staff, but also from concerns regarding the motivation for the purchase. Typically, even when such constraints are imposed, exceptions will be made for legitimate purchases.

Budget analyses. The starting point for the development of any budget is gaining an in-depth understanding of both the current budget and the preceding one. The most recently completed budget will provide valuable information about how resources actually were received and expended throughout the period. It will highlight shortfalls and indicate programs that may be in their downward cycle. It also will identify opportunity targets for increased investment—for example, units experiencing increased demand that shows no signs of tapering off. Examination of the budget for the current period will give early warning signs of potential problems and other issues that may require attention in the upcoming budget.

Typical issues examined through analyses include past experience with diverse types of revenue such as investment income, gifts, sponsored program, and other revenues that must be monitored centrally. Experience with expenses also is analyzed from a variety of perspectives. To the extent possible, it is desirable to analyze expenses to determine whether they can be projected more accurately based on various factors. For instance, if one can establish a strong relationship between a particular category of expenses and a generally available cost index, monitoring the cost index will provide an early indicator of changes in expense levels. This technique is common with healthcare costs, which are monitored using the Healthcare Cost Trend Rate to provide early warning of significant increases in premiums.

Planning. The importance of planning is emphasized throughout this book. As the budget development process begins, the results of the planning efforts must be considered along with information about past actual results measured against the budget. The combination of these factors will shape the upcoming budget. Areas of need should be evident from analysis of past results, while priority areas should flow from the planning process. The budget process will require extensive negotiation, and the presence of well-defined plans will make the process run much smoother. Not every decision will flow easily from the plans, but the absence of plans will make each decision a struggle.

Good planning processes involve participation by all campus constituencies, including the board. This element is key to the process because it creates a natural link at the board level between planning and budgeting. Active involvement of trustees is desirable in planning, but not in budgeting. The board influences the overall direction through their involvement in the planning process, and the budget is a primary tool for use by management in carrying out the plans. It would not be appropriate for the board to participate directly in the budget process.

Projecting enrollment. With the exception of a few enviable institutions with capped enrollment and excess demand, most colleges and universities will experience changes in enrollment from year to year. If institutions operate in a stable enrollment environment, this step likely will be omitted. Instead, those institutions will build the budget using the same enrollment numbers as in the past.

The vast majority of institutions, however, will invest a significant amount of effort attempting to predict enrollment accurately for the upcoming year. For tuition-dependent institutions, this process is crucial. The gain or loss of just a few students can have significant implications for the institution's bottom line. Even for those that are not as dependent on tuition as a source of revenue, predicting the number of students is a critical step because enrollment influences so many aspects of the budget. For this reason, the planning process will focus a good deal of attention on enrollment and related issues.

Many institutions—especially public institutions—are facing expanding enrollments each year. The number of graduating high school seniors is on the rise, and there are more nontraditional students enrolling in college. As a result, there is tremendous demand for education. Unfortunately, it comes at a time when many states are unable to provide the resources needed to cover educational expenses. Consequently, a significant amount of effort is invested in analyzing various data elements and the factors that influence enrollment to determine how many students are expected and how many can be accommodated.

In addition to the number of individuals seeking an education—the potential pool of applicants—pricing decisions affect enrollment. In fact, tuition discounting has become a very significant factor. Tuition discounting refers to the practice of offering institutionally funded aid to students beyond their demonstrated need. Essentially, the institution uses some of its resources to attract students who might otherwise not enroll. By offering even a partial scholarship, an institution can attract students with particular skills or qualities to fill a void in the expected incoming class.

In some cases tuition discounting focuses less on student qualities than on economics. Assuming that an institution has excess classroom and housing capacity, attracting a student by offering a partial scholarship results in an increase in net revenues. For instance, an institution charging $13,000 for tuition and $7,000 for room and board can realize approximately $15,000 of additional revenue if it attracts a student with a $5,000 scholarship. Although there may be some modest increased costs from serving an additional student, those costs are nominal compared with the additional revenue.

Developing assumptions. In addition to plans and other inputs such as enrollment projections, every budget must be built on a series of general assumptions. Plans describe what the campus seeks to accomplish; assumptions create the framework for the plans. Assumptions usually are developed by the budget office with input from other offices, including planning, admissions and financial aid (or enrollment management), institutional research, human resources, and the treasurer's office. The assumptions address issues such as the likely increase or decrease in enrollment by level; the expected inflation rate for various expense categories; planned salary increases for various employee categories such as faculty, administrators, and staff; and other factors that must be considered in the development of a budget. Once finalized, assumptions typically are presented for approval by the board.

Projecting central revenue. Departments have substantial influence over some revenue streams—especially at the graduate level. When considering other revenues—such as undergraduate tuition and fees, gifts, investment and endowment income, and even sponsored program recoveries—central offices are in a much better position to project revenues for the upcoming budget. As a general rule, the number of undergraduate students is established centrally for the entire institution, recognizing that they will be distributed among various colleges and departments. Therefore, central administration is in the best position to project tuition and fee revenues (along with financial aid expenses, which typically are addressed concurrently with tuition and fees).

Endowment and investment income generally will be addressed by the treasurer or controller. Endowment income typically is a firm number because most institutions employ a spending formula based on historical market values. Investment income, on the other hand, is influenced by several factors, including the budget itself. Investment income available for operating purposes usually is generated by investing idle cash balances in short-term investments. Cash balances fluctuate based on factors within the institution's control, such as the success in collecting receivables or managing the timing of expenditures and other disbursements, as well as factors beyond the institution's control, such as economic conditions and their impact on short-term investment rates.

Decisions made during the budget process also will influence the availability of cash. For this reason, the treasurer typically provides both an expected earnings rate and a range of revenue that is likely to be earned based on decisions made during the development of the budget. For instance, a budget that anticipates significant increases in reserves—institutional savings— will likely provide more investment income. On the other hand, a budget that anticipates spending from reserves will usually reflect reduced investment income.

Gifts can be a particularly difficult form of revenue to project—especially at smaller institutions lacking sophisticated development operations. Although many factors contribute to fund-raising results, it's generally true that the past is a very good indicator of the future. Absent major economic changes—positive or negative—or special fund-raising initiatives such as capital campaigns, most development officers are able to project giving levels with reasonable accuracy, especially in the area of unrestricted support. Using analysis of the most recent year, supplemented with current-year experience, it's possible to make reasonably accurate projections about what will happen in the coming year.

Overhead recoveries are another category of revenues that may seem difficult to project. In fact, it's not as difficult as one might expect. The vast majority of overhead recoveries for a given year will be a function of awards already received. Therefore, the starting point is the analysis of existing and pending awards. For smaller institutions with limited sponsored program activities, it can be difficult to predict expenditures from sponsored programs. It's also true, however, that in these situations the indirect cost recoveries are relatively small compared with the rest of the budget, so it is desirable to project revenues in a conservative manner. This strategy avoids the risk of overlooking a source while still protecting the institution against shortfalls. Over time, the experience gained through analysis will pay dividends as projections become more accurate.

Other miscellaneous central revenue sources vary from institution to institution, but one potentially significant revenue source is of particular interest to public institutions: state operating appropriations. Depending on the type of institution (e.g., research, doctoral, liberal arts) and the state, this revenue category may contribute as little as 8 percent or as much as 45 percent of all operating revenues. Understandably, it is crucial to have accurate predictions about the level of support expected from the state. In states that allow institutions to set tuition rates, the state operating appropriation usually is the single most important factor affecting those rates. Even in states that have not granted tuition-setting authority, the state's support will have a major impact on various expense categories—especially salaries and benefits.

The process of projecting state operating appropriations will vary from campus to campus based on several factors. A key consideration is the state's process for establishing its budget. In some states—especially those relying on well-defined formulas—the campus can project revenues based on other factors, such as enrollment, employment levels, and usable space. The formulas are applied using the projected data, the results are incorporated in the assumptions, and the budgets are developed accordingly. In other states, the process is much more fluid, and institutions are forced to incorporate more contingencies to protect against shortfalls in anticipated support.

Projecting expenses. Except in institutions relying on responsibility center management, central administration must make projections about expense categories. The two most significant categories are salaries and fringe benefits. Compensation represents the largest expense for higher education institutions. Despite significant investments in facilities, infrastructure, equipment, and technology, the annual depreciation and amortization charges related to these assets is modest compared with the expenses incurred for human resources. Compensation—consisting of salaries, wages, and benefits—can be as high as 70 percent of operating revenues.

The expenses for selected benefits can be tied directly to salaries and wages. Generally, any expense that is assessed as a percentage of salaries (for example, FICA, unemployment insurance, and worker's compensation) can be determined merely by applying the applicable rate to projected salaries (taking into consideration any ceilings that may apply). Other benefits, however, cannot be linked so easily to salaries. For instance, health insurance usually is the most expensive fringe benefit for higher education. Health insurance rates are negotiated annually and extraordinary increases have been all too common in recent years.

Another critical projection that central administration must provide is the inflation factor applied to various expense categories. In the largest categories, projections are addressed using specified percentage increases influenced primarily by institutional decisions. Other items, however, are subject to external influences beyond the institution's control. This information must be used to project the expenses that are affected.

Budget guidelines. To help departments develop their budgets—and to minimize the likelihood of unrealistic submissions—the budget office will provide instructions and forms to those responsible for the accounts and activities that will be reflected in the final budget. These guidelines cover a wide range of issues. Examples include enrollment trends and their implications for staffing; the distribution of tenured and nontenured faculty appointments; the distribution of part-time faculty; anticipated tenure and promotion decisions; anticipated sabbaticals; and the distribution of instructional workload for departments.

Processes vary from campus to campus, with more and more institutions relying almost exclusively on electronic submissions transmitted either via e-mail or an intranet. In these situations, the forms used in the electronic submissions typically will incorporate various edits and diagnostics to prevent submissions that are not consistent with the instructions.

It is still common, however, to rely on paper submissions using campus-developed forms. When the process is paper based, it's typical for the budget package to be routed to units through the applicable organizational layers so that management can add unit-specific guidelines. For instance, a dean may require that all departments in his or her college allocate a specific percentage for curriculum development. Or a major administrative unit may require that its departments identify a portion of their budgets that can be reallocated for special initiatives. At the department level, these types of guidelines may have greater influence on the budget than those imposed by central administration.

In addition to providing budget guidelines, it's typical for larger institutions to conduct training for those responsible for developing budget submissions. Some institutions use online tutorials and live workshops to convey the important aspects of developing a budget submission. It is interesting to note that campus personnel—including faculty and academic administrators—almost always find time to attend budget-related training, unlike training on many other administrative topics. Most individuals with budget development responsibility recognize that there is much to lose if they are not fully aware of the budget guidelines and procedures.

Preparing the budget submission. Ultimately, the department head is responsible for the unit budget submission. Depending on the size and complexity of the unit—and both unit and institutional policy—this individual may involve numerous others in the process or simply rely on the unit financial administrator. The larger the department, the more likely it is that faculty and additional departmental administrators will participate in developing the budget submission. For very large departments with significant amounts of gift support and sponsored programs activity, it's likely that several departmental administrative personnel will perform most of the work required to complete a budget submission. Conversely, for very small units the entire process may be handled by the department head with clerical support from a departmental secretary. The latter approach also is typical in situations relying on an incremental budget process.

Budget submissions are prepared at the lowest unit level and submitted for review and approval by successive levels of management—either electronically or through a manual process. At each step, the responsible individual (for example, division head, dean, and vice president) reviews the submissions to ensure that collectively they represent the best possible proposal for the unit. Once each level is satisfied that the combined budgets are consistent with the unit plans, address all identified priorities, and comply with relevant guidelines, the budgets are submitted to the next management level and finally to the budget office.

Consolidating the budget. The budget office accumulates all unit and central account budget proposals to develop the consolidated institutional budget, usually with some type of budget software. Automating the process enables the budget office to produce a consolidated budget as submissions are received. Thus, they can assess how things are coming together and spot any problems that materialize.

Sometimes budget software is a module in an administrative software suite, sometimes referred to as an enterprise resource planning system or ERP. With this system, the development and submission of budget proposals is streamlined using technology—frequently an intranet. This approach usually incorporates actual results from the current and prior years, providing additional context for the budget proposal.

An alternative approach might rely on stand-alone budget software such as SAS Financial Management, FRx Software's Helmsman, or Hyperion Pillar. Although highly automated and frequently utilizing an intranet, these tools are more likely interfaced to other administrative software such as the general ledger (the accounting system), rather than integrated with it. For this reason, stand-alone software may not incorporate as much historical information.

Not every institution has the capacity to employ automated solutions. At these institutions, the budget details must be loaded manually into whatever tool is used to produce the consolidated budget—a time-consuming and labor-intensive process. These institutions are less likely to produce preliminary consolidated budgets. Instead, they focus on entering all source information. Once everything has been received and processed, the budget is produced. A manual process is more likely to yield mistakes that must be corrected before an accurate budget can be produced. As such, significantly more time is required for manual processes—both for input and error correction.

Regardless of the method used and its level of automation, once the consolidated institutional budget has been produced, it must be analyzed to ensure that it is consistent with the institutional plan, that all priorities have been addressed, and that the final numbers meet the target established in the assumptions phase.

Budget review and approval. Once the budget has been finalized and the budget office has demonstrated to senior management that it supports the objectives outlined in the plan, management will submit the budget to the board for review and approval. Assuming the board was involved in the development of the institution's plans and approved the assumptions used to develop the budget—and that the budget is consistent with those plans and assumptions— board approval should not be a problem. In most situations, the board will seek assurance about specific issues identified during the planning process or request the identification of any special risk areas embodied in the budget. It's a good idea for management to anticipate these questions and provide supplementary narrative information. Once the questions have been answered and the board has had a chance to discuss the implications of the budget, final approval becomes something of a formality.

If, on the other hand, the board determines that the budget deviates from approved plans or assumptions in some way, they may withhold approval. Should that occur, management typically will direct the budget office to make the changes needed to respond to the issue or issues raised by the board. If the board remains unwilling to approve the budget, there is a more serious problem. The board and management need to invest the effort required to resolve the issues that stand in the way.

Budget implementation. Once the board has approved the budget—and ideally well before the beginning of the new fiscal year—the general ledger must be updated to reflect the new information. This step is necessary because various administrative processes must occur to be ready for the fiscal year. Depending on the closeness of the start of the academic year, it may be necessary to process new hires into the payroll system, issue purchase orders, or execute leases for rental space. In some cases, administrative systems will allow activity for a future year to begin in the current fiscal year. In other cases, however, the new budget must be loaded before spending commitments can be made. The earlier that the budget can be implemented, the better prepared the campus will be for the next academic year.

Operating Budget Calendar

It is not unusual to repeat certain steps for selected units because their budget proposals do not follow guidelines or achieve specific targets. Moreover, although it is rare for the board to reject the final proposed budget, it is possible. Depending on the board's reasons, it may take a significant effort to make the revisions needed to gain their approval.

For these reasons, it's essential that the budget calendar have sufficient flexibility to allow for the routine re-examination of individual components. The time period for the overall budget development activities will vary tremendously from one institution to another, but the entire process can take anywhere from six to 12 months at independent institutions, and appreciably longer at public institutions because of the influence of state agencies. The end point usually is keyed to the board's meeting schedule, so it's a good practice to include a month or more of cushion within the budget calendar. Failure to do this could necessitate the scheduling of a special board meeting for the sole purpose of reviewing and approving the budget. When this occurs, it's likely that the board will be much more inclined to examine the budget in greater detail than it would have if the normal schedule had been followed.

Every institution's goal is to have the budget approved as early as possible in advance of the start of the fiscal year. Ideally, approval should happen sufficiently early to begin the recruitment process for new positions. This step is crucial if new faculty will be teaching sections in the fall semester or if any other approved positions are expected to generate revenues during the year. Unless the revenue projections contemplate hiring delays, it is likely that there will be revenue shortfalls if the new positions are not filled early in the year.

Unfortunately, recent history at public institutions demonstrates that it is frequently difficult, if not impossible, to finalize a budget much in advance of the start of the fiscal year. It has been all too common in recent years for state legislatures and governors to be unable to reach agreement on the state's budget during the prescribed timeframe. Like the federal government, several states have operated with continuing resolutions, executive orders, or similar administrative stopgap measures to enable state government, including public higher education, to operate without the benefit of an approved statewide budget. Although temporary authorization allows public institutions to conduct most routine operations, it impairs effectiveness, stifles innovation, creates anxiety about the possibility that cutbacks may be needed later in the fiscal year, and frequently interrupts progress on construction projects. The latter situation is especially common when the capital appropriation is provided on a fiscal year basis rather than a project basis.

The overall situation is made even worse if the state's budget process includes the approval of tuition rates. Although normally a rare occurrence, there have been numerous instances in recent years in which public institutions were forced to raise tuition rates in the middle of an academic year because they were not able to establish rates for the fall semester.

Another problem unique to public institutions is some states' use of biennial budgets. It is desirable for institutions to employ multiyear budgeting as a means of managing operations more effectively, but this approach poses a hardship when it occurs at the state level. Too often, the state's budget cycle forces institutions to project far into the future—sometimes more than two years from the latest completed period. The discipline that accompanies such a model can be beneficial when a public institution chooses to use it internally. More often, though, it proves to be problematic because institutions have only limited influence with respect to what happens at the state level.

When projecting so far into the future, budgeters typically reduce the uncertainty by using current experience as a base. Adjustments are made at the margin to reflect anticipated changes in revenues and expenses, which in turn are determined by a host of variables, including program mix, enrollments, various market factors affecting the availability of job candidates, inflationary influences, and investment yields. Scheduled changes such as the introduction of a new degree program or tighter admissions standards can be planned for, but it is difficult to predict more extreme events such as new environmental regulations, dramatically changing interest rates, changes in federal student assistance programs, and the impact of national or international events. As a result, it is much more likely that public institutions operating in this environment will be forced to default to incremental budgeting and include significant contingencies as a protective measure.

Capital Budget Cycle

As with the operating budget cycle, there is wide variability in the specific steps included in the capital budgeting process. The typical capital budget cycle includes fewer steps generally but lasts appreciably longer than the operating budget cycle (see Figure 3-3). Operating budgets cover only the activities that occur over a one-year cycle. Although individual programs may continue for years (for example, a multiyear sponsored research project), and activities such as instruction will occur as long as the institution exists, the focus for an operating budget is a single fiscal year. Another factor differentiating capital budgets from operating budgets is the dollar magnitude of individual projects. Even a very large sponsored project usually will not represent as large a financial commitment as the typical project addressed in a capital budget. Similarly, it's not uncommon for an individual capital project's budget to exceed the combined annual operating budgets for a number of academic departments.

Projects covered in capital budgets range from the acquisition of a single major item of equipment, to the renovation of a laboratory, to the acquisition or construction of a campus building. Depending on institutional policies and procedures—and the volume of capital activity ongoing at any point in time—the capital planning and budgeting processes can be as complex as those for the operating cycle. For other institutions, with fewer resources available for capital activities, the processes may be relatively informal. At these institutions, only minimal formal planning may be undertaken. Instead, the institution might maintain a wish list of projects that will be undertaken as resources become available or in response to operational problems. Under these circumstances, it is typical for needed capital projects to be delayed until problems reach crisis proportions. For instance, despite recognizing that a roof is long overdue for replacement, an institution may choose to wait until leaks become too numerous to patch. This situation is discussed in greater detail in the "Deferred Maintenance" section.

A more desirable approach for capital planning and budgeting involves a formal process for identifying and addressing capital needs. The steps involved in such a process usually include the following.

Establishing need for space. The need for new space (or significant renovations to existing space) is identified at the department or school level. The unit develops the rationale for additional space, citing the specific activities that will be conducted in the space. The request might focus on increased sponsored programs activity, the introduction of a new academic program,

FIGURE 3-3

CAPITAL BUDGET DEVELOPMENT CYCLE FOR THE UNIVERSITY OF VIRGINIA

SCHEDULE FOR 2006-2012 SIX-YEAR PLAN

May 2004   Distribute call to vice presidents for 2006-2012 six-year capital plan and 2005 capital budget amendments.

July 2004   Amendment requests and project initiation forms due for each new project.

Prepare six-year plan and 2005 budget amendments.

Aug. 2004   Present six-year plan and budget amendments to executive review committee for review and approval. Emphasis is on 1) biennial plans, 2) project justifications, and 3) funding (state general fund, bond, gift funding proposals for each biennium; and, impact on student fees).

Prepare governor's budget amendments.

Sept. 2004   *Governor's budget amendments submitted to Commonwealth of Virginia Department of Planning and Budget.*

Oct. 2004   University architect completes project formulation documents for proposed projects.

Nov. 2004   Vice president for finance completes business plans and debt assessment impact for proposed projects.

Dec. 2004   Present six-year plan, business plans, and debt assessments and legislative budget amendments to executive review committee for review and approval.

Jan. 2005   *Legislative budget amendments for 2005–2006 submitted to Commonwealth of Virginia Department of Planning and Budget.*

Feb.2005   *Commonwealth of Virginia Department of Planning and Budget notifies agencies of submittal schedule for 2006–2012 six-year plan and unfunded projects from 2004–2010 six-year plan eligible for the preparation of detailed submissions.*

Mar. 2005   Six-year plan presented to special governing board committee for final review and approval.

Apr. 2005   *Six-year plan submitted to Commonwealth of Virginia Department of Planning and Budget.*

June 2005   *Detailed documents for projects approved by state in February submitted to Commonwealth of Virginia Department of Planning and Budget.*

Notification by Commonwealth of Virginia Department of Planning and Budget of six-year plan projects approved for detailed submittal.

Notification by Commonwealth of Virginia Department of Planning and Budget of maintenance reserve subprojects that meet required criteria.

Aug. 2005   *Detailed documents for projects approved by state in June submitted to Commonwealth of Virginia Department of Planning and Budget.*

Annual maintenance reserve plan documents submitted to Commonwealth of Virginia Department of Planning and Budget.

Sept. 2005   Complete financial feasibility studies for revenue bond projects.

Nov. 2005   *Governor submits six-year capital improvement plan to General Assembly.*

Dec.2005   *Governor submits 2006–2008 biennial budget to General Assembly.*

Jan. 2006   *Legislative budget amendments for 2006–2007 submitted to Commonwealth of Virginia Department of Planning and Budget.*

May 2006   *2006–2008 appropriation act approved by General Assembly and governor.*

July 1, 2006   Approved 2006–2008 project authorizations take effect.

Items in italics represent interactions with the state or activities that occur at the state level.

Source: University of Virginia Budget Office

improved faculty-student interaction because of technological upgrades, or enhanced campus-corporate training partnerships. The request usually includes an analysis of existing space resources and an explanation of why they are not sufficient to accommodate the new activities.

Search for existing space. Once the need has been identified and shown to be consistent with the institution's plans and priorities, a search is undertaken to see if any other space on campus can be reassigned to accommodate the need. If existing space can be reassigned without adversely affecting other institutional activities, this will happen. If it is determined that no existing space is available for the purpose, the process begins to acquire or construct space in which the activity can be conducted. Depending on the importance and urgency of the particular activity, it is possible that an interim arrangement will be made to rent space.

Campus master plan review. After the addition of new space is approved in concept, it is necessary to review the campus master plan to determine the appropriate location for the space. Master plans address long-term facilities and infrastructure needs and identify how the physical space will be developed over time. An effective master plan, covering a 10- to 20-year period, will guide a campus as it develops its physical resources to maximize their programmatic benefit and aesthetic value and also assure that financial resources invested in facilities and related areas provide the maximum benefit possible. Plans typically are reviewed and revised on a regular basis and rewritten approximately every 10 years.

Campus master plans identify specific areas reserved for academic expansion, along with the designated location for any new residential facilities, administrative space, athletics and/or recreation venues, and other buildings. Within the constraints of the institution's political climate, it is typical for a master plan to indicate areas of potential boundary expansion for the campus. This issue obviously is a sensitive one, and, in some situations—especially at independent campuses—it is not included in the plan. Public institutions, however, usually must disclose expansion plans even though it may lead to difficult relationship issues with the local community. Unlike most independent institutions, public institutions are subject to open meeting/open records laws and regulations requiring that official actions taken by the board or management be open to the public. This burden is somewhat offset by the fact that a public institution may be able to resort to eminent domain to acquire land in support of its mission. Under eminent domain, the public institution directly, or through the local government, forces the transfer of privately owned land to the institution (with appropriate compensation to the owner). This is a last resort; it is much more typical for public institutions to acquire land through normal competitive purchase.

Feasibility assessment. Only in rare circumstances will a campus undertake space acquisition or construction to address a single need for space. More typically, this need will be combined with other identified needs to determine the best overall solution. It may be desirable to acquire an available commercial facility, or it may make more sense to construct a new on-campus facility. The decision to buy, lease, or build will be made after considering various factors, such as the suitability of available commercial space; the overall cost comparison between building/leasing new space and acquiring and renovating commercial space; the availability of space that can be rented until a permanent solution can be implemented; and the time needed to construct the needed space.

Obtain needed approvals. The next step in the process is to obtain the approvals required before a capital transaction can occur. The effort required to obtain approvals will vary dramatically between independent and public institutions. As a rule, approval of land or other significant capital acquisitions (such as those above a certain dollar threshold) at independent institutions occurs only at the board level. Except in rare circumstances, no one outside the institution is required to authorize the institution's acquisition of capital assets. (In some unique situations, an independent institution seeking to acquire land locally must obtain approval from the local municipality. The approval usually is linked to concerns regarding the property tax implications that arise when a tax-exempt organization acquires property and removes it from the tax rolls.)

The approval process for public institutions is much more substantial and requires significant lead-time. Most states have statutory requirements related to the acquisition of land and/or buildings. Various state agencies will be required to approve the acquisition or construction of new facilities. In some states, this only occurs if state funds will be used to finance the acquisition or construction while, in others, all transactions must be approved at the state level. Along with concerns related to demonstrated need, there also are environmental considerations such as asbestos or ground contamination, building and related construction code regulations, and other issues related to public policy. If the transaction requires debt financing, additional approvals will be required from various state financial offices.

Acquisition or construction. Once all approvals have been obtained, the purchase is consummated or the actual construction begins. Depending on the nature of the project, this may take several years. During this period the capital budget will be reviewed on a regular basis to assure that the overall capital portfolio is being managed effectively. Cost overruns are common with construction projects, and it is not unusual for an individual budget to have a sizable contingency factor. The amount will vary from project to project, but 5 percent is customary, and some budgets may contain a 10 percent contingency.

Deferred Maintenance

Another important issue related to budget cycles is the method for addressing deferred maintenance. This term refers to the scheduled routine repair and maintenance of facilities that is postponed, thereby creating a backlog. Every campus has some amount of deferred maintenance resulting from various operational considerations. A particular classroom facility may be due for interior painting but, because of increased demand for the program housed in the facility, the decision is made to postpone the painting until spring break during the following academic year. Or a roof that is scheduled to be replaced must continue in service due to the temporary unavailability of required specialized materials. Situations like this are not problematic when they are short-term.

On the other hand, many institutions have very large backlogs of deferred maintenance that have developed because of financial stress. In other words, revenue shortfalls or expense overruns in prior years have prevented the institution from making the repairs or conducting the maintenance in accordance with the established schedule. A modest deferred maintenance backlog may be manageable, but once it grows and becomes too large to be addressed within normal operating cycles, the overall condition of facilities begins to deteriorate rapidly. Even relatively new facilities will operate suboptimally if not properly maintained.

For these reasons, institutions seek to quantify the deferred maintenance backlog so that it can be addressed through the operating budget, the capital budget, or both. Normal repairs and maintenance are considered to be an operating expense. As such, they typically are addressed by including an amount in the operating budget to address at least a portion of the backlog. And if the institution is able to end the year with unanticipated surpluses, it's common to allocate a portion of the surplus for addressing the backlog.

When the backlog becomes greater than what can be accommodated routinely through the operating budget (or surpluses it generates), it frequently must be addressed through the capital budget. In this situation, the capital budget includes a special category to address various critical aspects of deferred maintenance. The major concern for such projects is the funding source. It is unlikely that bonds can be sold to finance deferred maintenance projects, so it is typical that other sources must be found. Many public institutions receive special appropriations for this purpose. Independent institutions, however, must generate the funds themselves through operating surpluses or through fund raising.

Whatever mechanism is used to address a deferred maintenance backlog, it is important to pay attention to this issue. Unlike many other indicators of financial stress—such as reduced enrollment resulting in declining revenues, increased bad debts from students not paying their bills, or increases in accounts payable due to liquidity problems—deferred maintenance backlogs do not appear in audited financial statements. The effects of deferred maintenance may be visibly apparent, but there is nothing in generally accepted accounting principles requiring that the amount of the backlog be disclosed. Administrators must ask the right questions to ensure that the backlog does not become unmanageable.

As important as it is to monitor deferred maintenance backlogs, it's even more critical to take steps to prevent the growth of deferred maintenance. Attending to existing backlogs poses a financial challenge, and the problem becomes worse as new facilities are added. The campus building boom of the late 1990s and early 2000s creates the potential for significantly increased deferred maintenance burdens. One strategy being employed by a number of institutions is to place a moratorium on new facilities projects unless they come with a dedicated renewal and replacement reserve for the facility. In other words, the source of ongoing maintenance funds must be identified at the start of any new capital project. This will assure that new facilities do not contribute to the deferred maintenance backlog. Obviously this approach addresses only part of the problem because it does not generate funds to address the existing backlog. Still, it is a step in the right direction.

chapter four

ALLOCATING RESOURCES AND INCREASING FLEXIBILITY

I ndividuals who are not involved in the budget process frequently won-
der what they can do to influence the allocations made through the
process. Specific questions can be asked about the process itself: Who
should participate at each stage? Is the budget driven by a plan, or is it
merely a continuation of what was done the prior year? What information
has been the most useful to current participants? How can the timing be
revised to enable more thorough analyses of the critical factors affecting the
institution? Or questions can be asked about the outcomes of the process:
Should tuition and fees be increased for next year? If so, by how much?
Which departments should receive increased resources next year, and which
ones should experience reductions? What are the implications for fringe
benefits if salaries are increased by 2.5 percent? Over time, participants
become more skilled at raising the right questions in the appropriate manner
so that they have the maximum possible impact on resource allocations.

Another frequently asked question, especially by those with day-to-day
responsibility for planning and budget management, is, "How do I deploy
the institution's resources to maintain the maximum amount of flexibility?"
Flexibility is essential to be able to respond to changing circumstances and
conditions. It is inevitable that things will not always play out as projected.
One way to provide flexibility is through contingency funding. Some expenses may prove to be larger than expected. Major winter storms may
drive snow removal costs beyond anything that might have been considered
possible. The contracted Internet service provider may go bankrupt, forcing
the institution to rely on a back-up provider with rates originally set only
for short-term consumption. A faculty member may need a substantial
commitment of institutional matching funds to secure a major research
project. Any of these situations could occur. Without adequate contingency
funding, they can wreak havoc on resource allocation plans.

Apart from contingency funding, maneuverability is a key element supporting flexibility. For example, funds with the fewest restrictions on their
use can be held back and not allocated at the outset so they can be available to address unanticipated issues. State general funds usually cannot be

used to finance facilities projects above a certain dollar threshold, whereas unrestricted private resources can be used to cover cost overruns on such projects. Flexibility comes from allocating state general funds to qualified activities and preserving unrestricted gifts and unrestricted endowment income for support of activities that are not eligible for state funding.

Another critical issue is risk tolerance. The greater the institution's aversion to risk, the more important it is to develop a budget that provides maximum flexibility through contingency funding and maneuverability. Flexibility is a way to avoid undue risk. Not allocating all anticipated resources to committed expenses or investments is a way to avoid incurring the risk that resources will be insufficient to meet the commitments. A budget that allocates all anticipated resources runs the risk that some planned expenses or other investments will have to be deferred due to revenue shortfalls or cost overruns.

The best opportunity to influence the budget is at the planning stage (see chapter 3). Some of the most important budgetary decisions actually occur during the planning process, an essential activity that should precede the budget process and be linked with it. To wield meaningful influence, a participant should be involved in both the planning process and the budget process. The major decisions that influence resource allocations are both process related and content related. For instance, resource allocations are affected just as much by which institutional representatives participate in the process as they are by the actual amount of resources available for allocation.

Participants generally expect that they can affect the way in which resources are distributed if they analyze the institution's programs and activities in a logical, orderly manner. The issues raised in this chapter provide a framework for analytical thinking. Still, it is important to recognize that politics cannot be overlooked or underestimated in weighing the budget outcomes. The political environment and the spheres of influence of members of the college or university community vary from campus to campus. Through friendships with trustees or legislators, a department chair may have political connections that give him or her influence far beyond that normally indicated by such a position. An administrator or faculty member who has participated in the budget process over many years may gain knowledge of the institution and accumulate enough political debts to become a powerful figure during budget negotiations. Some participants are more articulate than others and therefore enjoy greater success at garnering resources. In general, the more complex the budget process and the greater the individual interconnections, the more complex the political environment becomes. The framework presented in this chapter shows how institutions can strike a balance between rational planning and the inevitable political maneuvering.

This chapter identifies the major issues common to most colleges and universities that affect resource allocation. Recognizing that relatively few institutions have effectively integrated planning with budgeting, this chapter also suggests the stages in the budget process during which the issues typically are addressed. Significant attention is paid to budget flexibility and to three elements that should have universal applicability: the academic plan, the allocation of faculty positions, and the enrollment plan.

The first section revisits the concept of institutional character. The second section covers the importance and the sources of budget flexibility. The third section examines several key planning components that have significant influence over the budget process. It reviews academic, administrative, and revenue factors that can be addressed to affect resource allocation decisions. It also suggests ways for faculty and administrators to question the basic assumptions on which budgets are constructed. It includes a discussion of the potential hidden costs of administrative and programmatic decisions and examines external administrative and revenue factors that influence the budget.

The issue of influence is discussed by raising questions in four areas: the budget process itself; academic and administrative policies and procedures; revenue estimation techniques; and the hidden costs of some activities. The final section covers some strategies that decision makers use to allocate resources while maintaining maximum flexibility.

Institutional Character: The Environmental Factors

Institutional character is an amalgam of elements that, when taken together, describe an institution's uniqueness (see chapter 3). Institutional character is often reinforced as a result of inertia, primarily because of tradition and the tendency for most large organizations to resist change. Participants in the budget process should not expect significant changes in an institution's character in a single budget cycle. Nevertheless, using the budget is a wonderful way to effect change.

One can argue that the relationship between the budget and institutional character is a "chicken-and-egg" proposition in that they tend to influence each other. Resource allocation decisions are frequently driven by institutional character; similarly, that character is in many ways a function of past resource allocation decisions. An institution can change its character, albeit slowly, by changing the way in which resources are allocated. It is important to recognize that few such decisions will, in and of themselves, bring about major change, although some will provide a stronger push than others. For instance, an institution that is not noted for its research proficiency may make great strides in a relatively short period simply by establishing and staffing a small office of sponsored programs. Moreover, if this step is coupled with the establishment of an internal initiatives fund, used to provide seed money to faculty interested in pursuing sponsored support, the institution can move from a position of little to no external support for research to measurable results within a few short years.

Recently a number of colleges and universities have attempted to change their character through intercollegiate athletics. Several have chosen to change divisions within the NCAA classifications. In most instances, the movement is to a higher, more expensive category. In a few cases, however, institutions have decided to drop a sport or move to a classification requiring less investment. Each action creates an opportunity for the institution to change its character. Sometimes the change can be very dramatic.

There are times in an institution's evolution when it is primed for major change or transformation. This type of change can be thrust upon the institution by external forces, or the impetus for change can come from within the institution. In either case, astute observers will recognize the presence of these opportunities and use the budget process to achieve specific objectives.

A number of factors may create an opportunity for dramatic changes in institutional character. The institution may experience a significant shift in enrollment patterns or greater demand for some programs than for others. For instance, current social and political events may influence students to pursue some disciplines in numbers far exceeding typical patterns. When it becomes clear that the shifts are more than a short-term phenomenon, the institution will use the budget to realign resources to meet the demand.

Changes in employment demographics may also alter an institution's character. The country is about to experience a dramatic increase in employee turnover as the baby boom generation approaches traditional retirement age. In addition, the tenure of presidents and other senior administrative officers has shortened dramatically in recent years. The combination of increased retirements and more frequent leadership transitions results in significant opportunities for changed institutional character.

Economic changes may also signal an opportunity for major change. The 1990s was a period of tremendous endowment growth for many colleges and universities. Although relatively wealthy institutions with large endowments did not necessarily experience changes in institutional character, others seized the opportunity to reshape themselves in dramatic ways. Many with modest endowments were able to increase the endowments to a level at which they could provide significantly greater financial resources than ever before. In some cases, this situation was used to change the overall character of the institution.

Significant changes can lead to broad readjustments of resource allocation patterns. Therefore, it is essential to understand the institution's character and seek to recognize shifts as they occur. It is important to note that shifts may not always be obvious, so it is wise to pay close attention to factors that are more easily monitored. Such tangible factors as academic plans, administrative priorities, and revenue fluctuations can be tracked easily from year to year and adjusted when necessary. Over time, changes in these factors also will influence institutional character, but typically in a more manageable way.

Budget Flexibility

Planning has been mentioned as the key factor in any budget. Unfortunately, the activities and programs offered in higher education do not lend themselves to detailed, accurate plans. In addition, it is unlikely that the variances will allow unmet revenue targets to be offset by better-than-expected expense results. To accommodate this reality, effective budgeters build flexibility into their plans in anticipation of significant changes in revenue or expenses. One mark of a well-regarded institution is its ability to take advantage of unforeseen opportunities and respond to unanticipated problems. Budgets must be as flexible as possible if they are to respond to unanticipated situations. An unanticipated windfall of funds is rare, but a wise budgeter will know in advance how to deploy such resources as soon as they are identified. In fact, at the institutional level, the plans should include a list of priorities to be addressed if resources become available— either through unanticipated savings or through a windfall.

At each level of the budget process, participants have the opportunity to budget every potential resource to its fullest or to reserve a cushion that can be used to respond to expense overruns or revenue shortfalls. The cushion built in at the department level is modest but will allow the unit to respond to issues that might arise. More cushion is needed at the highest levels because of the magnitude of the issues that might be dealt with. An increase in the cost of a special laboratory supply may affect only one or two units and probably will be accommodated with even a modest amount of cushion. On the other hand, a major spike in energy cost, such as that experienced in California in the early part of the decade, can absorb the entire contingency reserve.

Flexibility usually is structured according to the portion of the budget to which it pertains. Compensation costs account for as much as 60 to 70 percent of most college or university budgets; fixed expenses such as utilities and physical plant maintenance represent approximately 10 to 15 percent. The balance usually is spent for operating expenses such as service contracts, technology, supplies, communication, noncapital equipment, and travel. Typically, constraints on the use of funds differ from one expense category to another. For example, in many institutions, amounts budgeted for compensation may not be spent for other operating expenses. Instead, amounts not spent are captured centrally for reallocation or, in some public institutions, must revert to the state. Strategies for creating flexibility tend to be tailored to the activity, the expense constraints affecting the institution, and the level of operation within the institution.

To some, the concept of flexible resources has a negative connotation of inefficiency and poor administration. Contingency funding in an institutional budget is sometimes considered "fat." One extension of this philosophy is the notion that a leaner budget translates into greater accountability or improved efficiency. In fact, the most effective organizations are those in which resources can be marshaled as necessary to respond to challenges or take advantage of opportunities. Most budgeters recognize the importance of flexibility and will seek to protect the budget contingencies from those above and below in the hierarchy. They must take care, however, not to go to extremes by forgetting that the contingency funds are there to be used when needed. They should not be spent unwisely, but neither should opportunities be missed because of a misguided desire to build reserves at all costs.

Managers typically seek to shift uncertainty to others. Department heads routinely turn to deans or central office personnel for resources needed to respond to emergencies or opportunities. For instance, a department that encounters unanticipated price increases for needed supplies or higher-than-expected salary demands for an adjunct needed to replace a faculty member who becomes ill may expect the provost to provide supplemental funding to address the situation. Conversely, deans and central administrators may take on the burden of monitoring departmental spending closely to anticipate problems, or they may use their contingency funds to address problems within departments rather than use them for opportunities at the college level. State officials often shift uncertainty to public higher education systems or to individual campuses by establishing regulations that prohibit operating deficits.

The notion of flexibility changes from one budget cycle to another as circumstances change. New resources must be found to adapt to different conditions, and new strategies must be utilized to create contingency funding in the budget. Although budgeters at all levels seek to include cushion in their portions of the budget, they are reluctant to label it as such for fear that others may seek to claim the amounts.

Changes in revenues or expenses arise from five primary sources:

+ Enrollment fluctuations

+ Revenue fluctuations

+ Expense fluctuations

+ Emergencies

+ Unforeseen opportunities

The uncertainty surrounding enrollment projections is a major reason for building cushion into the budget. If enrollments fall below expected levels, institutions will lose tuition and, in the case of public institutions, may lose state appropriations as well. Unless the expense budget contains a cushion, the institution will face a deficit for that year. Similarly, excess enrollment can create budget problems. Additional class sections may be required to accommodate the unanticipated increase in enrollment, but the revenue generated from the enrollment may not be sufficient to cover all additional costs. Unanticipated enrollment increases may also affect auxiliary units. It usually is not a problem for dining operations, but bookstores may not have adequate textbook inventories to meet demand, or there may not be sufficient campus housing for the additional students, who will be crowded into existing space.

A different problem occurs when enrollment patterns do not follow historical trends. For instance, enrollment may shift dramatically among majors in such a way that it is not possible to reallocate resources. It may become necessary to engage adjunct facutly to meet the increased demand even though no savings can be realized in the programs that experience enrollment drop-off.

Revenue shortfalls in sources other than tuition and fees can cause budget problems. Investment income may not meet targets due to unanticipated market conditions. Adverse publicity may cause donations to decline. Similarly, economic problems within the state might affect state revenues, thereby causing the state to reduce appropriations to public institutions. If the problem develops late in the fiscal year, it may require the institution to return funds already received.

Expense fluctuations also can have significant impacts—even when they do not rise to the level of an emergency. An unanticipated postage hike, increased insurance costs due to a spate of natural disasters, and price increases for repair materials used in the physical plant are examples of expense increases that, if experienced simultaneously, could create a significant deficit requiring attention. Campuses are like small- or medium-sized cities. Price increases in almost any commodity will affect them. If the increase relates to a widely used commodity, the impact can be significant.

The types of emergencies that can adversely affect a college or university vary widely. Several years ago, when the federal government overreacted to an indirect cost issue, many campuses were forced to repay amounts that had been collected as part of the normal overhead recovery process related to sponsored agreements. In some cases, the amounts were significant and were required to be remitted on relatively short notice. The California energy crisis mentioned earlier resulted in major budgetary disruptions for colleges. Although most campuses have several types of insurance, a natural disaster can strike at any time and cause an institution to incur significant unplanned expenses to meet policy deductibles. Many would argue that the dramatic price increases in health insurance constitute an emergency. Typically, these events cannot be anticipated when the budget is planned 6 to 18 or more months prior to its implementation. The best that budgeters can hope for is to have sufficient reserves, provide adequate contingency funding, or have the freedom to alter other budget plans to accommodate these situations when they arise.

Ultimately, flexibility comes from having adequate revenues to conduct activities and programs. Unrestricted revenues such as tuition and fees, unrestricted gifts and endowment income, some state appropriations, and surpluses in auxiliary or other self-supporting activities provide the resources that cushion an institution against unforeseen events. The critical task is identifying the cushion and preserving it despite the demands of daily operations. Strategies for the creation of resource reserves are discussed later in this chapter. The strategies themselves are shaped in large part by the key decisions made during the planning and budget processes.

Key Planning Components That Influence the Budget Process

Influencing the budget process can be viewed from two complementary perspectives: the identification of key decision points that afford the greatest opportunity to influence the budget with the least investment of time and effort, and the development of a series of strategies that give the budgeter as much flexibility as possible. There are three specific opportunities to exert significant influence on the budgeting process: during updating of the institution's academic plan, when faculty positions are allocated, and during enrollment planning.

Academic Plan

Many colleges and universities do not engage in strategic planning but rely exclusively on an academic plan. However, the academic plan really is a component—albeit the largest one—of the strategic plan. In the best of circumstances, decisions concerning resource allocation are guided by program priorities. The priorities for academic activities are established through the academic plan. Priorities for support activities generally flow directly from the priorities identified in the plan.

Academic planning follows a different timetable and process from budgeting, sometimes making it difficult to draw direct connections between the two. Budgeting is cyclical, with a predictable schedule as outlined in chapter 3. Academic planning is less regular and occurs when an institution identifies the need to examine program priorities and possibly shift direction. The time required to complete an academic plan usually will exceed that of a single budget cycle. A budget developed in the midst of an academic planning cycle might represent a continuation of past priorities rather than move the institution toward the direction identified in the planning process.

The participants in academic planning may not be the same individuals involved in the budget process. Although there may be some overlap between the groups, this tends to be the exception rather than the rule. The problem with this approach is that those charged with developing the budget frequently lack an in-depth understanding of program priorities and their origin. The result of this disconnect is likely to be missed opportunities.

Academic planning requires divergent thinking so that different program options can be explored, resulting in revised priorities. Budgeting requires convergent thinking to match available resources to identified priorities. The differing timelines also create the need for different approaches. Budgets are focused on a 12-month period, even when multiple years are budgeted at one time. Because academic plans take time to develop and implement, the planning horizon is usually much longer—typically five years or more.

The linkage between academic planning and budgeting should come from the use of the planning process outcomes—the academic plan—as the framework for budget decisions. Conversely, outcomes from the budget process should inform the academic planning process. These linkages help ensure that the academic plan for the early years is linked to the reality of the existing financial environment. Academic plans differ widely in their specificity. As with budgets, there is no standard format.

Participating in the academic planning process provides an opportunity to influence the institution's resource allocations—though perhaps not as directly as participating in the budget process. Still, effective budgeting is guided by the outcomes from academic planning. Because the academic plan sets the framework for decisions about resource allocation, it becomes a significant decision point related to but outside of the budget process. The academic plan influences multiple budget cycles, so those who help to develop it may have a greater impact on resource allocation decisions than participants in a single year's budget process.

Allocation of Faculty Positions

The most important resource for any academic institution is its faculty. Regardless of how an institution accounts for that resource—whether numbered positions with authorized salary ranges or a lump sum that can be used to employ any number of faculty—the decision about the distribution of vacant faculty positions or dollars that can be earmarked for faculty hires is the most important decision that can be made about resources. The decision is even more significant if an allocation of support money (for staff, supplies, telecommunications, and other items) goes along with each faculty position. Although resources for faculty positions are included in the budget, these decisions often are made outside of the budget process—when program changes occur, hiring opportunities arise, or the departure of a faculty member forces an immediate hire.

Before decision makers can allocate faculty positions, they must have a systematic way to establish them. A new position can be created only if sufficient resources are available to cover compensation. The resources might come from tuition, endowment income, state appropriation (frequently tied to enrollment), or other sources that are not otherwise committed. Non-endowment gifts typically are not used to support a new faculty position because the position usually represents an ongoing commitment. Unless the situation is unique (for example, a visiting scholar), most institutions will require the identification of an ongoing revenue source, such as tuition or endowment income, before creating a new position. Existing faculty positions can be vacated through retirements, resignation, death, tenure denial, or a decision not to renew the contract of a nontenure-track position. Decisions related to vacant positions are just as critical as those related to new positions (unless it is the institution's practice to allow departments to retain faculty positions when they become vacant).

Most institutions have a hierarchy of decision-making authority for the allocation of faculty positions. In one model, the chief executive or chief academic officer controls all faculty positions. All new and vacant positions are pooled, and units must submit requests, supported by justifications, to the appropriate official. As an alternative, faculty positions may be controlled at the school or college level. In this case, the department heads or research directors submit requests for faculty positions to the dean of the college or school. Requests typically relate only to position vacancies, since new positions usually are established only with approval from the highest level—either the president or the provost. Occasional exceptions involve endowed chairs, but even in these cases the central administration must authorize acceptance of the gift that funds the position.

Enrollment Plan

Many institutional resources, especially in the instructional and student services arenas, are allocated in response to the number of students that must be served. Clearly, the number of students and their distribution by school, college, or program are important considerations. The more sophisticated and accurate the enrollment projection and enrollment management models, the more control campus decision makers will have over the allocation of resources.

The development of a campus enrollment plan, based on predictions of acceptance rates for applicants and retention rates for current students, usually occurs on a different schedule than that of the budget process. The enrollment plan in the aggregate must be connected to the budget process because it will influence estimates of tuition and student fee revenues, enrollment-driven expenses such as faculty salaries, and buying decisions made by auxiliaries such as the bookstore and dining services.

Shaping the Policy Environment for Budgeting

Participants

Many questions about the budget process focus on the degree of participation by various constituents. Budget reviews can involve budget staff and administrators or be expanded to include faculty, students, and other constituents. Constituent groups may take part in the process through a variety of mechanisms, including advisory committees and budget hearings. The effectiveness of the review process will be influenced significantly by the quality of individuals chosen to participate, their level of institutional knowledge coupled with the support they receive from budget staff, and the willingness and ability of the budget office to provide data in a form that will facilitate a meaningful review.

The degree of openness in the review process will be determined in large part by the institution's culture. Colleges with small faculties and staffs and a strong sense of shared governance will probably have relatively open deliberations. Large institutions, or those without a highly participative governance structure, will more likely have a relatively closed budget process without much input from constituents. Generally speaking, a more open process is desirable. There are tradeoffs, however, between open and relatively closed processes.

The more open the process, the harder it is to ask the difficult but necessary questions that arise during the process of making resource allocation decisions and negotiating levels of support. On the other hand, the criteria for distributing resources may be more widely debated and understood if the process is open. The opposite tends to be true of closed processes.

The question of departmental roles illustrates the pros and cons of participation in the budget process. Should departments have a role in developing the budget, or should central budget office personnel have sole responsibility? Among other factors, the answer depends on the kinds of expectations the institution wishes to encourage among departments. For example, if the institution will have insufficient revenues to satisfy requests for additional resources, the decision to involve departments may have the disadvantage of raising expectations that cannot be met. On the other hand, if the institution has a culture of openness and inclusiveness, involving departments has the advantage of ensuring that the best information about resource needs is available. With this approach, requests and justifications are based on information that might not otherwise become available to participants at later stages of the budget process. As departmental staff and faculty become aware of the constraints, their expectations may become more realistic, creating an opportunity to build consensus regarding direction.

When faculty or students participate, there generally is a formal campus procedure for selecting representatives. The nature of the participation (advisory or decision-making), the elements of the budget subject to review, and the timing of the review must be specified in advance. How each of these factors is addressed influences the outcome of the budget process. For instance, selecting constituent representatives by voting may yield the most active participants, but they may not be the ones best able to judge programs and activities.

Another factor that affects which individuals should participate is the nature of the budget elements under review. Reviews that focus solely on academic budgets may not properly address administrative and support activities essential to academic units' success. The timing of participation and the amount of time allotted for review will influence the effectiveness of the participation. Participants must have sufficient time to review the materials and consider alternative allocation decisions. The resulting recommendations will be more useful to policy makers at higher levels if they are available well in advance of the time when decisions must be finalized.

The benefits of an inclusive process must be weighed against the risk of negative outcomes. Not having input from students or faculty may result in suboptimal decisions. On the other hand, involving them and not accepting their input likely will be worse. If an inclusive process is the goal, it must be recognized that meaningful participation will necessarily take more time. In addition, a successful process is explained carefully to manage the participants' expectations. If the process is not well understood and it produces recommendations that are unrealistic or impossible to implement, the effort is likely to produce more negative results than if no involvement had been allowed.

If budgeters are willing to sacrifice the privacy of their deliberations for the sake of broader knowledge of review criteria, they generally have some assurance that the information will be communicated accurately to members of the academic community. Still, budget participants in large institutions often find that communication channels are unreliable and transmit distorted or incomplete information. Similarly, the give-and-take of budget review may sometimes generate mixed signals, especially if negotiations occur over an extended period. What was true at one stage of the process may no longer be true as the process approaches its end.

It is important to distribute information about the status of the budget throughout the process—especially to lower-level units that may not have direct access to decision makers. Departments or colleges often submit their budget requests at the beginning of the process and receive only limited information before seeing a final budget approved by the legislature (in public institutions) or the governing board (in independent institutions). In this situation, the departments have no idea about their success in making a case for additional resources or how their requests were perceived relative to others in the institution. With the Internet, there is no excuse for failing to disseminate information regularly.

Academic and Administrative Policies, Procedures, and Practices

An important way to influence the pattern of budget decisions is to alter the policies and procedures related to the allocation and use of resources. Because compensation represents the largest expense category, this area is the first to consider.

A useful framework for considering changes in a budget takes into account three factors:

+ Increases or decreases resulting from inflation or deflation

+ Increases or decreases related to workload

+ Improvements in or deterioration of the quality of a program or activity

Inflation or deflation factors reflect changes in the prices of goods and services, including cost-of-living adjustments to salaries and wages. Changes in faculty workload usually reflect changes in enrollment, demand for course offerings, the number of courses and sections taught, or the volume of sponsored activity. Changes in administrative and staff workload mean changes in the level of service provided or the number of activities being undertaken. The third factor accounts for qualitative variations among programs and activities. A decision to decrease average faculty instructional workload might be made with the expectation of either enhancing the quality of instruction or improving the volume of research. Another approach could be to improve instructional quality or the effectiveness of faculty advising through enhanced technology. Applying the three factors to budget review enables decision makers to be more discriminating in adopting budget strategies and more accurate in projecting the consequences of those strategies.

Programmatic directions. The first step in examining the budget is usually to identify major issues and establish priorities for academic and support programs and activities. The academic plan is the framework that facilitates this review. Ideally, resources should be allocated to encourage or promote selected activities according to established priorities. If, for example, research is identified as a priority, departments that are successful in attracting external research funding may receive increased allocations for positions and funds to allow increased faculty release time. If higher enrollments are the objective, academic departments that increase their enrollments may receive additional faculty positions or increased support costs per

FTE faculty position. If the objective is to increase the use of instructional technology, at least two actions are likely. First, the units supporting faculty in these efforts will receive additional financial resources. Second, the individual faculty pursuing enhanced technology in their teaching will be at the top of the list for upgraded personal computing. In each of these examples, the budget is the mechanism for signaling what is important. And in each case, the signals actually should emanate from the planning that shaped the budget. Participation at the planning stage is likely to have the greatest impact.

As budgeters review the plans to gain an understanding of program priorities, they also attempt to identify the means for measuring progress. Typically, the measures are a combination of quantitative indexes (such as student-faculty ratios, student credit hours per FTE faculty position, and square footage maintained by physical plant) and qualitative indicators (such as the quality of a department's faculty, national reputation of a department, and service orientation of support units). Not all indicators lend themselves to quantification, so professional judgment must always be applied.

Each policy and procedure discussed in this section must be considered in light of three factors.

- The extent to which the quality of the activity or program is being improved

- The extent to which the activity is responding to a change in workload or demand

- The extent to which the purpose for the activity is being altered (diminished, expanded, or redirected)

Teaching loads. A college or university's single most important resource is its faculty. In allocating resources to departments, most institutions consider some measure of instructional workload. Four of the most common indicators are student-faculty ratio, average student credit hours per FTE faculty position, faculty contact hours (weekly time spent in the classroom or lab), and number of courses taught. Departments with larger credit-hour loads have higher student-faculty ratios and generate, on average, more student credit hours per FTE faculty position. To determine the policy implications of these ratios, one must also consider the effect of the class size on teaching loads (and, more important, on instructional outcomes). Class size and instructional methodology also will dictate the relationship between faculty contact hours and student-faculty ratios. Generally, the indicators are best used as a basis for initial analysis of the instructional process, not as the sole basis for allocation decisions.

Departments that depend more heavily on laboratory or studio instruction will have lower ratios than departments that rely on large lectures. Questions can be asked about the extent to which departments depend on labor-intensive instruction:

- Is there an opportunity to alter the mix between laboratory instruction and large lecture?

- Does the discipline require individualized instruction, as in the case of studio training for musicians?

- Do accreditation standards mandate certain instructional methodologies?

- Is it possible to respond to increased student demand by relying more heavily on instructional technology as opposed to adding additional faculty positions?

Individual faculty teaching loads vary widely even within a single department. Within a given department the following questions, reflecting policy options, can be raised:

- Are faculty with lighter teaching loads given reduced loads as a matter of tradition or policy or because they are more active and productive as scholars?

- Are faculty teaching loads skewed by rank? For instance, are senior faculty required to teach only two courses per semester while assistant professors must teach three? If so, does this practice prevent the junior faculty from competing effectively for sponsored research funding?

- Do faculty members with equivalent credit-hour production actually have comparable workloads? For instance, is one individual teaching large lecture sections of only two courses while another is teaching several different courses with fewer students per class?

- Do some faculty teach the same courses year after year, or are course assignments rotated throughout the department?

In addition to answering questions like these and making interdepartmental comparisons, it is helpful to conduct trend analysis of departments' workload over time. An appropriate balance may have deteriorated either because of increased demand without additional resources or reduced enrollments without a corresponding reduction in staffing. It is also beneficial to consider all factors when attempting to make interdepartmental comparisons. There may be legitimate reasons for differences between seemingly similar departments. For instance, some disciplines enjoy increased opportunity for sponsored support. If the faculty in those departments are successful in attracting grants, their success will affect instructional ratios for the department.

Weighting factors for teaching loads. Faculty positions frequently are allocated based on measures of instructional load. Typically, the measures consist of elements weighted by level of instruction or level of student. Weighting is skewed in favor of advanced levels of instruction and students under the theory that effort at higher levels is more time consuming for faculty and therefore more expensive. The relative difference among weights also may reflect institutional priorities regarding instruction at various levels. For instance, lower-level undergraduate courses might be weighted at 1.0, upper-level undergraduate courses at 1.5, graduate instruction at 2.0, and graduate research at 3.0. These particular weights, which may be totally arbitrary, assume that a faculty member engaged in research involving graduate students is investing three times as much effort as a faculty member teaching a lower-level undergraduate course. Although instructional effort varies by discipline and even course, these variations usually are ignored, and weighting is applied uniformly across the curriculum.

If the weighting used to compute teaching load is indicative of institutional priorities, any revision in the weighting should reflect a change in priorities. If resources are allocated based on weighted student credit hours, for example, a change in weights will lead to a change in the distribution of resources. Figure 4-1 demonstrates how a change in weighting in favor of graduate instruction and research can alter the distribution of resources. Under the existing weighting, even though Department A is producing more unweighted credit hours, Department B is entitled to more faculty positions because it is producing relatively more hours at the graduate level. Changing the weighting in favor of graduate effort results in an even greater disparity in the number of positions assigned to Department B. This change could be the result of a change in priority or the result of analysis indicating that the revised weighting more accurately reflects the relative effort required at the various levels.

FIGURE 4-1

ILLUSTRATION—FACULTY STAFFING AS DETERMINED BY WEIGHTING FACTORS

(Assume 1.0 FTE faculty position carries a load of 600 weighted credit hours.)

	Credit Hours by Level of Instruction	Current	Revised	Weighted Credit Hours Current	Revised	Net Increase
Department A						
Lower division	3,000	1.00	1.00	3,000	3,000	
Upper division	4,000	1.50	1.50	6,000	6,000	
Graduate instruction	1,500	2.00	2.50	3,000	3,750	
Graduate research	500	3.00	3.50	1,500	1,750	
Total	9,000			13,500	14,500	
Divide by full-time load				600	600	
# of FTE faculty positions				22.5	24.2	1.7
Department B						
Lower division	2,000	1.00	1.00	2,000	2,000	
Upper division	3,000	1.50	1.50	4,500	4,500	
Graduate instruction	2,500	2.00	2.50	5,000	6,250	
Graduate research	1,000	3.00	3.50	3,000	3,500	
Total	8,500			14,500	16,250	
Divide by full-time load				600	600	
# of FTE faculty positions				24.2	27.1	2.9

Distribution of faculty ranks. Departments with a higher proportion of junior faculty typically are less expensive to support because salaries are lower. In addition to the fiscal implications of the distribution of faculty by age and rank, there are several academic considerations:

- Is the distribution of faculty expertise within a discipline or department appropriate for its instructional and research missions?

- Is the proportion of tenured faculty low enough to provide for the periodic addition of "new blood"?

- Are the guidelines for promotion clearly communicated?

- Do tenure and promotion criteria differ significantly from one department to the next? How are exceptions handled when there is an opportunity to recruit a faculty "star"?

- Are vacant positions filled at the same rank as that of the former incumbent?

Faculty demographics cannot be changed quickly, even with dramatic changes in policies and procedures—especially when a substantial percentage of the faculty are tenured.

Distribution of faculty salaries. The distribution of faculty salaries will vary from one department to another for a number of reasons, each of which has implications for budget policy. These questions will guide the consideration of salaries:

- Does the distribution of faculty salaries correspond to faculty ranks?

- Is the distribution of faculty salaries more closely aligned with seniority than with the faculty's contributions and professional accomplishments? What incentives and disincentives result from the answer to this question?

- How large (or small) is the gap between salaries for new hires and those with long service? What factors have influenced this gap, and what are its effects on faculty job satisfaction or the ability to recruit qualified faculty?

- Do the differences in faculty salaries across disciplines reflect market conditions?

The salary distribution issue typically arises when a department seeks to fill a vacant faculty position, especially one in the senior ranks. A common strategy is to fill vacant senior professorial posts from among current junior faculty. The benefits of this strategy are that the salary savings can be invested elsewhere; the junior faculty are encouraged to remain with the institution because there is upward mobility; and the department is able to replace the junior faculty with an outside hire, thereby introducing "new blood" into the unit. This approach is not without problems, however. Unless the junior faculty member being promoted is capable of providing the leadership lost with the senior faculty member's departure, the department may suffer. A department staffed primarily with junior faculty needs senior leadership to be able to respond to the challenges that arise. If the person promoted cannot provide it, any benefits from salary savings or improved morale among junior faculty may be offset.

A common concern of faculty at all ranks is how the salary adjustment pool is determined. In the aggregate, salary adjustments are tied to the expected increase in institutional resources. Typically, tuition, endowment income, and appropriations provide the resources needed to cover all increased operating expenses, including salaries. The salary increase usually consists of two components: a merit pool and an across-the-board, or cost-of-living, adjustment. Some institutions add a third component. This pool is used for special recruitments, to retain a faculty member recruited by another institution, or to provide salary increases for faculty promotions.

In many public institutions the cost-of-living adjustment is determined at the state level and applies to all state employees, including faculty. There is no national standard for the size of the salary adjustment pool or the split between merit and cost-of-living adjustments. Colleges and universities tend to invest more dollars in the merit pool to create the opportunity to reward individual performance. The recent history of salary increases is second in importance only to resource availability among the factors influencing the size of the salary increase pool. When resources are available, an institution that has been unable to provide competitive salaries will attempt to remedy this situation as quickly as possible. Similarly, if an institution is attempting to increase its salary ranking among peer institutions, it is likely to invest more in salaries than in other operating expense categories.

In most cases, the merit adjustment pool is calculated as a percentage of total salaries and distributed to each academic and administrative unit for assignment to individual faculty and staff. If the chief executive officer, chief academic officer, or deans reserve a portion of the institution's total salary adjustment pool as a contingency fund, selected pro rata departmental allocations may be supplemented to remedy disparities among departments in terms of market conditions or institutional priorities.

Use of part-time and temporary faculty. As budgets become tighter, more departments and institutions depend on part-time and temporary faculty to stretch their dollars. Generally, these faculty members receive considerably less compensation and benefits than permanent faculty members. In addition, it is not unusual for temporary or part-time faculty to be ineligible for many benefits, thus increasing the savings. Another advantage of relying on part-time faculty is that they can be hired only when needed based on student demand.

There is a downside to excessive reliance on part-time or temporary faculty. First, although many adjuncts are excellent instructors, others are not as skilled as permanent faculty. Because of the relatively low compensation they receive, there is no incentive to invest the extra effort to enhance their skills. In addition, they typically have relatively heavier course loads than permanent faculty, leaving little time for their own scholarly pursuits. Part-time faculty also tend to be less available to students and colleagues because of their other employment activities. Finally, because of the lack of commitment on the part of the institution, many part-time faculty will go to the highest bidder for their services, jumping from one temporary position to another.

Many institutions establish policies controlling the employment of part-time or temporary faculty. In some institutions, part-time faculty can be hired only with funds budgeted for this purpose or with savings from vacant permanent faculty positions. In other institutions, there are prohibitions against using permanent faculty position vacancy savings to hire part-time faculty. Some of these policies are driven by collective bargaining agreements, but others evolve from an institutional desire to rely on full-time faculty to the maximum extent possible. There are many policy questions related to part-time and temporary faculty:

- Should departments have the latitude to hold faculty positions vacant solely to provide resources for temporary hiring?

- Is there a proper balance between instruction provided by permanent faculty versus part-time faculty, especially at the undergraduate level?

- How are savings realized from the utilization of part-time or temporary faculty? Do they support the department's instruction, research, or service activities, or are they captured centrally?

Public institutions in particular must exercise caution when it comes to part-time and temporary faculty. First, some states closely monitor the status of permanent employee positions. If a department attempts to maintain vacancies for the purpose of employing part-time or temporary faculty, the permanent position might be eliminated in a subsequent budget because of state action. In addition, many states are reacting to complaints from some undergraduates about the excessive reliance on part-time or temporary faculty by placing limits on the number that can be employed in a given period. Still other states set a cap on the overall faculty head count. Excessive reliance on numerous part-time faculty may cause an institution to exceed the cap.

Sabbatical leaves. Many institutions have a sabbatical leave policy for faculty that provides one year of leave at half salary or one semester at full salary for every 6 to 10 years of full-time service. Some institutions award one-semester sabbaticals every seventh semester. For faculty leaves of one year, departments use the salary savings to employ part-time instructors to cover the permanent instructor's courses or pay overload to current full-time faculty. Any surplus is used to cover other departmental needs. Arrangements that allow for full pay during one-semester sabbaticals tend to be costly for departments because there is no savings available to pay part-time faculty. Practices may vary from one department to the next as long as the institution's overall policies are followed. Common questions related to sabbaticals include the following.

 • Are sabbaticals guaranteed for all faculty meeting the minimum service requirements?

 • Are faculty expected or required to seek outside funding to cover part of the sabbatical leave?

 • If one-semester sabbaticals at full pay are permitted, are the faculty member's classes canceled, or are other arrangements made (such as temporary instructors employed to teach the courses or overload payments to other permanent faculty)?

Graduate assistants. In institutions offering graduate instruction and relying on graduate assistant positions for teaching or research, practices vary widely among departments. Graduate assistantships offer significant flexibility in staffing departmental responsibilities. Graduate assistants might be used as graders, lab section coordinators, instructors of independent sections, or research assistants. In addition to issues around specific roles for graduate assistants, there is the matter of how the assistantships are allocated throughout the institution and within departments. Among the various models are those based on seniority, on the percentage of teaching load represented by large lecture classes, and on scholarly or research productivity. Another approach is simply to allocate the positions across the board based solely on enrollment.

Support staff. The distribution of academic support staff (for example, clerical workers, laboratory technicians, and grants specialists) may vary significantly from department to department. The differences may result from specific instructional methodologies, the nature and extent of research activities, instructional loads, service commitments, or simply historical patterns. A key consideration is whether there should be institution-wide standards for these positions. An important aspect of this issue is the increasing reliance on technology for clerical support. Many support positions have been eliminated with the advent of the personal computer. Once the hardware and software costs have been covered, what happens to the savings represented by the elimination of the positions?

Administrative and student support. The academic portion of the institutional budget cannot be understood without analyzing its relationship to the administrative and student support budgets. If the academic mission (instruction, research, and service) is primary, academic and student support budgets should be developed primarily to facilitate activities in the academic arena. Over time, however, support activities can become ends unto themselves. For this reason, many campuses have established requirements for periodic reviews of support units to ensure that they effectively support the academic mission.

The following are examples of the types of questions that should be considered when reviewing support activities:

- Is the service essential to the campus?
- Does the service that this support unit provides duplicate services available from other units?
- To what extent are new technologies (such as automated systems) or approaches (such as outsourcing and shared services) being utilized to reduce the overall cost of the service and/or improve its effectiveness?
- Have performance standards for the service been established, and are they monitored on a regular basis?

A different set of questions is appropriate for auxiliary enterprises:

♦ Are the activities self-supporting?

♦ Are they expected to pay a fair share of the institution's operating expenses, such as utilities and accounting services?

♦ Are the units able to generate and maintain reserves adequate to meet operating needs, including facilities maintenance and expansion?

Physical plant operations represent an expensive aspect of a campus's activities. Questions relevant to physical plant operations include the following:

♦ Has the campus achieved all possible savings related to energy utilization?

♦ Does a preventive maintenance plan exist for all campus facilities?

♦ Is deferred maintenance measured on a regular basis and assessed with respect to its appropriateness given the current operating environment?

Student affairs is unique among support and administrative areas because of its direct involvement with an institution's primary constituents: the students. When reviewing student affairs, answers to the following questions may be enlightening:

♦ Do on-campus housing policies support enrollment plans and contribute to auxiliary units' success? For instance, are freshmen required to live on campus and, if yes, also required to purchase a campus meal plan?

♦ Are the offerings for student entertainment inviting so that students are encouraged to stay on campus, thus avoiding potential problems with the surrounding community?

♦ Does the campus use residential colleges led by faculty principals or language houses as a means of supplementing formal instruction with extracurricular activities?

Operating expenses. Academic and support departments and activities can be evaluated in terms of how effectively they use their resources for day-to-day operating expenses such as travel, supplies, and services as well as for small equipment. The following questions might be used to assess departments' performance in this area:

- Are units held accountable if they overspend their operating budgets?

- Does the institution have a mechanism enabling units to carry forward unspent funds from one fiscal year to the next (to avoid creating an incentive for units to waste money late in the fiscal year rather than appear not to need it)?

- Are units periodically asked to reallocate a portion of their existing budgets to a central pool to provide funds for higher-priority initiatives?

- Are travel funds allocated to faculty based on a clearly defined methodology?

Multiyear budgeting. The number of budget cycles influences the perspective taken during the budget process. Attention to one budget cycle, focused on a single fiscal year, leads to short-term thinking primarily related to incremental changes from the current year's budget. Expanding the process to focus on two to three years encourages a more proactive approach. Understandably, years two and three will have less detail, but they can be useful for highlighting shifts in priorities and broad institutional changes. For instance, if an academic program is being phased out over time, with resources allocated to other units, this activity can be reflected in the early budgets for the transition years.

Budget format. Another process-related issue is the format used for budget assembly and presentation. In most public institutions, the state dictates the format. Although it may be more efficient to use the same format for internal budget purposes, it is also likely that the state's prescribed format does not match well with the needs of an academic institution. For this reason, most public institutions operate with higher education-specific formats for internal budgeting and then aggregate the detailed information to comply with the state's prescribed format.

In both public and independent institutions, it is appropriate and desirable to assess periodically the structure of the budget and the types of information it contains. As with financial statements, budgets tell different stories. A budget that has functional or programmatic expense categories such as instruction, research, and institutional support will not have the same structure as one that displays expenses in natural categories such as salaries, benefits, and travel. The combination of the two formats generally is recognized as the most beneficial for decision making.

Related questions about budget format address issues about all-funds budgeting versus unrestricted funds only. Undoubtedly, it is easier to focus only on the unrestricted funds, but this approach is distorting and tends to result in suboptimal spending and management decisions. All-funds budgeting focuses on all resources received by the institution. It allows an institution to concentrate on the full magnitude of its operation, not just tuition and state operating appropriations. By relying on a single consolidated budget and a comprehensive process to manage and control operating resources, an institution will have the best opportunity to assure that priorities are established effectively and funded adequately.

Revenue Sources

Budgets are shaped by available revenues as well as by changes in academic and administrative policies and procedures. How revenues are projected, how institutional priorities are set, and institutional policies and procedures all exert influence over the budget and the budget process. In both public and independent institutions, student enrollments—and tuition pricing decisions—are the most influential determinant of revenue. Endowment income, though significant for some institutions, represents a modest portion of total revenue for the vast majority of colleges and universities. In even the wealthiest institutions, it is rare for endowments to contribute as much as 25 percent of total operating revenues. Another important though relatively small revenue source is nonendowed gifts. For some institutions, research yields a significant percentage of total revenues, especially when overhead recoveries are included in the measurement. Most research support, however, must be used for the purposes specified in the award and is not available for general operating purposes. Even overhead, though unrestricted, is a recovery of costs already expended and usually is committed for specific purposes.

Enrollment projections. Projecting student enrollment is more art than science, although many believe it is managed more effectively today than ever before. In the past an institution that projected enrollments accurately either was at maximum capacity or understood its potential audience and successfully controlled a number of key variables, including acceptance rates, student retention rates, tuition levels, and the overall attractiveness of its academic programs. Enrollment management has become increasingly complex, leading to the establishment of several consulting firms that specialize in assisting institutions with the task of recruiting students to maximize net revenues and to achieve the desired student body characteristics.

Numerous factors go into the determination of an institution's potential applicant pool, not the least of which is the institution's character, which will shape the kinds of questions to be addressed in this area:

+ What is the target population, and what institutional characteristics help define that population?

+ What information is known about the target population, and how can this information be leveraged to improve the results of student recruitment?

+ Can the target population be expanded either to grow enrollments or to enhance the quality of the student body?

+ How can the institution's character be modified to make the institution more attractive to potential applicants? For instance, what new programs can be added? Can additional housing be built? Should the institution switch from Division I athletics to Division II or vice versa?

As the competition for students has increased, advertising and recruitment campaigns have become more aggressive. Although some states prohibit their public institutions from engaging in student recruitment marketing, others recognize that the benefits of attracting the best entering students may make this practice a wise investment. Questions about this issue include the following:

+ Should the institution employ its own publicity staff, or should it contract for advertising services?

+ What kind of advertising and marketing should be undertaken, and where should it be directed?

+ How can faculty, alumni, and current students be involved in recruitment efforts to enhance the overall results?

Every institution has a pool of applicants, which will overlap with pools of other institutions. The objective for each institution is to attract the most desirable students within that pool. Applicants are screened by the admissions office and perhaps by a faculty committee, which evaluates each candidate according to institutional acceptance criteria. Because many potential students apply to multiple institutions, an institution is unlikely to admit all those who are accepted. As a result, enrollment projections must be based on a firm understanding of the historical acceptance and matriculation rates and the confidence that nothing will prevent the institution from achieving similar results in the future. When major changes in institutional character occur—such as the elimination of the requirement for lower-division students to live on campus or significant revisions in acceptance criteria—or if there is a significant change in economic conditions, the acceptance and matriculation patterns may no longer hold true. In addition, enrollment projections must also be adjusted to reflect overall trends in changes in student load or persistence. Clearly, the number of entering students is crucial in terms of its impact on tuition and fee revenue and, for most public institutions, state appropriations as well. Questions to consider include:

+ If the number of students offered admission is too low, are admissions standards too demanding?

+ If the number of students offered admission is too high, are admission standards too lax?

+ To what extent will more attractive student aid packages help to improve acceptance and matriculation rates?

+ Are life experiences appropriately credited in evaluating candidates for admission?

+ What special requirements and obligations are associated with equal opportunity in the admissions process?

+ Are transfer students encouraged to apply?

+ Are admittance rates for transfer students adjusted to compensate for changes in the admittance rates of first-time students?

+ Is sufficient effort invested in retaining current students?

+ Is course availability and scheduling an impediment to students' progress toward their degrees? For instance, is it possible to complete a four-year program within four academic years?

Admission to graduate programs is usually treated differently than admission to undergraduate programs. As a result, a different set of issues must be explored:

+ Is admission to graduate programs administered by an office of graduate admissions or by individual departments?

+ Does the office of graduate studies control the allocation of admissions slots by department and program? If not, are departments free to admit as many qualified students as they can attract?

+ Who determines the criteria for admission to graduate programs? Who is authorized to make exceptions to the criteria?

- Are the financial aid or graduate assistantship packages attractive to prospective students?

- How are sponsored program training awards integrated with admissions policies to ensure that qualified students are admitted to take maximum advantage of such awards?

One aspect of enrollment projections is estimating the number of matriculated students who will continue at the institution through graduation. Over time, a retention history evolves that is used to guide the projections. Students remain or depart from institutions for any number of reasons, including financial need, academic performance, family demands, and employment considerations. Because it makes sense financially and, presumably, academically to retain as many students as possible, many institutions have begun investing significantly in programs designed to enhance student retention. Budgeters should ask questions about these programs as well:

- Are the programs achieving the desired results?

- Is an analysis of the relative cost of the programs being conducted against their success?

- Are data being gathered for use in helping prevent students from departing before earning a degree? Is this information being shared with faculty to determine what changes might be needed in academic programs?

Tuition and financial aid. A key variable in the determination of revenues is net tuition (tuition minus institutional financial aid awarded to students). Tuition levels typically are established in close relationship with enrollment projections, expectations about nontuition revenues, and assumptions about overall expenses. In today's environment, another major variable must be added to the mix: institutional financial aid. Tuition usually is thought of as the published rate charged to students. In many cases—especially at independent colleges and universities—the published tuition rates bear little relationship to the amount of net revenue actually received due to the significant increase in aid being awarded to attract students. The process of setting tuition prices and institutional aid budgets has become an iterative one requiring consideration of investment returns, expectations regarding gifts available for scholarships, appropriations (for public institutions), and the overall budget picture. The following questions should be asked when reviewing a potential tuition increase:

- What impact is the increase likely to have on enrollments?

- Is there a price point at which a tuition increase actually reduces net revenue?

- How much should competitors' tuition rates be considered in setting tuition rates?

- How much should federal financial aid programs be considered in setting tuition rates?

- Is variable tuition pricing an option? That is, should tuition rates vary based on the demand for particular programs, student class level, or the costs of instruction—particularly for high-cost programs?

- Assuming that a public institution has the authority to set tuition levels, how much extra, if any, should be charged to out-of-state students?

- What is the appropriate relationship between undergraduate and graduate tuition?

- How should institutional financial aid be factored into the determination of tuition?

- Should tuition be determined independent of other fees, such as housing and dining?

When determining tuition levels, a key consideration is the amount of net revenue that will be realized per student. This factor is particularly important for smaller institutions, at which even a modest change can have a dramatic impact on faculty and staff positions as well as basic services.

Student fees. In most institutions, student fees are determined in combination with tuition. Setting fees for services such as dining, housing, and parking can be more complex than setting tuition because more factors need to be considered. Although competition and overall resource needs must be considered when setting tuition levels, the range of issues related to other student fees is much broader. Obviously, operating costs must be considered, but so must other issues, such as working capital reserves, facilities maintenance reserves, costs of holding inventory (especially significant for bookstores and dining services), and fluctuating employment levels. Because student fees are the primary revenue source for auxiliary units, and these units must operate as self-supporting businesses, setting fees or prices is critical. Nevertheless, the business needs of an auxiliary unit cannot be allowed to push the overall cost of attendance to levels that result in decreased enrollment.

Apart from auxiliary enterprises, student fees also provide resources needed to fund student activities such as intramural sports, student government, student clubs, and counseling and student health clinics. In some cases such fees pay for student access to intercollegiate athletics events. Other fee assessments are related more directly to academic activities, such as laboratory fees for courses taken in certain programs, technology fees, and special fees for individual music lessons or models for studio art programs.

Public institutions may have a unique opportunity when it comes to setting fees. Although it is not unusual for states to control tuition rates, they do not usually control fees. In fact, in some states where tuition is heavily controlled and fees are not, the combined value of fees assessed to students may be significantly larger than the tuition paid. Some public institutions that control the setting of fees but not tuition rely on fund transfers from auxiliary units for resources to cover some needs of academic units. This practice has been especially common in recent years when states have reduced appropriation support for campuses while preventing them from raising tuition rates.

Endowment income. The 1990s saw tremendous growth in institutional endowments as a result of increased giving and significant market returns. Although the situation has turned around in the early years of this decade, endowment income remains an important source of revenue. The typical budgeter does not have direct involvement with endowment management, which is handled by the institution's treasurer, by a committee of the governing board, or, in many public institutions, by staff at an independent fund-raising foundation. Nevertheless, many policies related to endowments and endowment income concern budgeters:

- ◆ What are the investment objectives for the endowment? Are they focused primarily on current yield or long-term growth? Too much emphasis on either one can be problematic. Current yield is needed to provide resources for operating expenses, but growth is essential to maintaining the endowment's purchasing power.
- ◆ Is there a clearly defined asset allocation strategy?
- ◆ What is the rate of return on the portfolio? How does this rate compare with the returns for endowments of similar size?
- ◆ What is the spending rate and how is it calculated?
- ◆ Are procedures in place to ensure adequate support for programs and activities even if the endowment returns are negative in a given period?

Other policy issues relate more specifically to the income generated by the endowment:

- How is income from unrestricted endowments utilized? Is it primarily used to support continuing operations, or is some or all of it used as seed money for new initiatives?

- How much of the endowment income is set aside to respond to contingencies?

- Is there any type of institutional matching program designed to encourage individual units to solicit new endowment gifts under which the income will be matched by institutional resources or the state?

- What portion of the endowment is restricted by donors, and is this taken into consideration when unrestricted revenues are allocated throughout the institution?

Gifts. Many colleges and universities receive significantly more revenue from annual giving than from endowment income. Gifts are less predictable than endowment income because the amount of endowment income available for spending in a given year usually is determined using historical data. Nevertheless, an effective development operation can predict gift revenues with a reasonable degree of accuracy using analysis of past giving patterns and known plans for future periods.

- Does the institution have a process for measuring the cost of fund raising? If yes, does the institution measure the success of fund raising against the investment made to generate gifts?

- Does the institution pursue multiple gift strategies, including annual giving, major gifts, planned gifts, and other methods?

- How much fund-raising effort is expected of individuals not working directly in development? For instance, are deans, department heads, and individual faculty members expected to participate in development activities?

- Does the institution maintain an alumni affairs office? If so, how closely is this office integrated with development?

- For religiously affiliated institutions, is the church a significant source of revenue?

- For public institutions, what is the relationship to the affiliated fund-raising foundation? Does the foundation determine how it will support the institution, or is this responsibility shared with institutional management?

Sponsored program funding. Sponsored support is another category that can be difficult to predict with a high degree of accuracy. Nevertheless, institutions for which sponsored programs represent a significant revenue source focus attention on this area and, in most cases, have developed sophisticated models for predicting the volume of revenue to be received. A key factor in predicting future revenues is that, in most cases, awards are received in advance of the period in which funding is received. This is especially true in the case of multiyear awards, which may be for as long as five years.

Predicting the direct revenues from sponsored activity may not be critical for some institutions because, in most cases, the funds are committed to a particular project and may not be used for other purposes. (Accurate predictions are still important, because amounts funded from sponsored sources may provide budgetary relief for other unrestricted budget resources.) Even when institutions are not overly concerned with direct revenues, those with significant volumes of sponsored activity usually are very interested in budgeting accurately the indirect cost recoveries that accompany such funding. In most instances this revenue represents unrestricted funds that can be used for any operating purpose. In theory, the funds are provided to reimburse the institution for overhead expenses incurred in support of sponsored activity. In practice, however, recoveries sometimes are used for a variety of purposes, including seed funding for young investigators, lab equipment, stipends for graduate assistants, supplemental funding for research libraries, and other objectives that may or may not be connected directly to sponsored activities.

The questions to be asked regarding sponsored support focus on two general areas: policies regarding activity outside the institution—particularly that involving the federal government, the largest sponsor and the most influential participant from a regulatory standpoint—and policies related to the conduct of research and the use of overhead recoveries.

- What are the current federal research priorities?

- Are the institution's academic activities aligned with those priorities? If not, is it possible to shift priorities to compete more effectively for this funding?

- How significant is the institution's technology transfer activity, and does it lend itself to partnerships with business, industry, or governmental entities?

- Does the institution have a mechanism to support investigators' pursuit of nongovernmental sources of sponsored funding (such as foundations and corporations)?

119

◆ What are the institution's practices relative to overhead recoveries? Are they captured centrally and treated as another revenue source? Or are they allocated throughout the institution to support additional research initiatives? For instance, some institutions routinely allocate a percentage of all overhead recoveries to the principal investigator or his or her department as an incentive to stimulate additional research.

◆ Does the institution allow overhead waivers to reduce the cost to sponsors when unique circumstances justify them?

Hidden Costs that Limit Flexibility

No one likes surprises—especially those with budget responsibility. Budgeters seek to limit the impact of surprises as much as possible. The most typical system is to budget contingency funding that can be reallocated to meet unanticipated expenses, provide funds to take advantage of new opportunities, or allow the institution to withstand revenue shortfalls. Even with contingency funding, however, some policy decisions carry hidden costs. For instance, the addition of a new facility involves construction or acquisition costs, and institutions rarely fail to acknowledge these costs. However, the ongoing operation and maintenance costs that will be incurred once the new facility is placed in service occasionally are not addressed. In addition to ongoing operating costs, funding is needed for new equipment and furnishings. Again, so much attention usually is focused on the facility that it is possible to ignore or underestimate some of these related costs.

Similar problems occasionally arise with the introduction of new academic programs. The obvious costs—salaries and benefits for new faculty and staff, space needs, workstations, supplies, and so on—are anticipated and factored into the budget. But the less obvious items—the cost and revenue impacts of the new programs—may not be addressed. For instance, if the new program attracts more students, it is likely that complementary programs will experience increased demand for their courses and need to hire additional instructors. On the other hand, the new program may not significantly increase enrollments in existing departments, but instead cause students to transfer from existing departments to the new one. The net result may be that courses in existing departments become undersubscribed, causing those departments to be overstaffed. A key consideration related to these examples is who should provide the resources to meet the increased or shifted demand for instruction. More than one department must bear the burden of curricular changes that affect several programs. There is no single right answer to the question, but the obvious implication is to ensure that all costs—and lost revenues—are considered before making programmatic changes.

The elimination of activities or programs may have hidden costs that erase some or all of the anticipated savings. For example, academic programs that require courses or services from the program being eliminated will have to find substitutes or provide the services themselves. If personnel are being released, reduction-in-force policies may require that the personnel displace other, less senior staff or be provided significant severance payments. Space usually is at a premium on campuses, so any vacated space will be in high demand. Nevertheless, there are situations in which unique, single-purpose space is abandoned as a result of program curtailment. Even if there is no need to invest in ongoing maintenance for the space once it is no longer in active use, costs will be incurred at some point to convert the space to alternative uses.

Human resource decisions can have significant cost implications if they involve positions protected by tenure or job security addressed through collective bargaining agreements. One cost is the loss of budget flexibility. Job permanence makes it difficult for budgeters to reallocate positions from one activity to another or to reduce the number of positions assigned to an activity. Moreover, tenured positions require a significant financial investment. If one assumes that an assistant professor is tenured and promoted at age 30 and continues to serve until age 70 at an average salary of $60,000 throughout his or her career, the decision to grant tenure represents a financial commitment in excess of $3 million for salary and benefits.

Hidden costs also may be a factor when new programs or activities are initiated with seed funding from grants or other temporary sources. Once the program or activity is operational and the seed money has been consumed, unless the program is able to generate resources on its own through gifts, service fees, or tuition, it may be necessary to support the activity from other resources. Higher education is not noted for its ability to terminate programs or activities, so once a program is established, it is likely to continue even if anticipated revenues do not materialize. It is a good idea to prepare for the possibility of a new program not generating sufficient funds to sustain it. Recognizing and accommodating these potential costs at the beginning will avoid problems in the future.

Strategies for Allocating Resources and Increasing Flexibility

The Regulated Environment: Constraints and Opportunities

Financial transactions in both public and independent institutions are governed by an array of accounting, human resource, and procurement policies and procedures, in addition to federal and other sponsor regulations. Independent institutions have more control over internal policies and procedures than do public institutions, which usually must adhere to guidelines applicable to state agencies. Even with the flexibility enjoyed by independent institutions, the combination of professional standards and federal guidelines tend to mitigate any competitive advantage. In addition, collective bargaining agreements in both the public and independent sectors affect budget flexibility.

Accounting policies and procedures. The complex structure of accounts that many institutions use is designed to assure that funds can be monitored and used only for appropriate purposes. For example, colleges and universities—especially many public ones—are precluded from using funds budgeted for salaries and wages for purposes other than compensation. Other categories of operating expenses may enjoy greater spending flexibility, especially in situations that do not rely on line-item budgeting.

Accounts or funds frequently are established to monitor specific revenue sources to ensure that they are spent for specified purposes. For instance, sponsored agreements have special rules related to the use of the resources. Similarly, proceeds from bond issues typically must be spent for specific capital projects. If an institution assesses special fees for certain activities such as laboratory work, student activities, or technology, the institution may require that these revenues be accounted for in specific funds so they can be matched against investments in these activities.

The degree to which faculty and staff actually comply with accounting policies and procedures is assessed by internal, independent, and—in some cases—federal auditors. Auditors examine not only the accuracy of management reports and financial statements but also the appropriateness of expense transfers, the support for expenses, and the overall internal control structure.

Anyone with budget responsibility must understand several aspects of the accounting structure. What is the nature of the expenses that can be charged appropriately to a specific account? To what extent can funds or expense charges be transferred between accounts? Does the fund structure within the institution impose constraints on the use of some resources?

Human resource policies and procedures. Because salaries and wages account for so much of an institution's budget, it is reasonable to expect that a large part of a budgeter's flexibility will be influenced by the institution's human resource policies and procedures. Contract and tenure obligations represent long-term financial commitments. The manner in which faculty salary structures are established and the ease with which adjustments can be made strongly influence the institution's competitiveness in recruiting faculty. Similarly, support staff salary structures, whether based on market conditions, union pay scales, or statewide public employee scales, affect the ability to hire and retain qualified staff.

Contractual and tenure policies specify the lengths of probationary periods, the amount of advance notice required for termination of an appointment, schedules for performance review, and grievance procedures. In some states these schedules are prescribed by regulation, and budgeting clearly depends on them. Moreover, the policies governing the appointment of temporary and part-time personnel will determine some of the constraints on budget flexibility. Faculty research appointments frequently may parallel tenure-track appointments but not require a tenure commitment. This flexibility is beneficial in the area of sponsored programs when timeframes may dictate quick-response hiring.

Procurement policies and procedures. Procurement regulations are intended to facilitate the efficient and economical acquisition of goods and services. As with most bureaucratic procedures, their complexity makes it hard for faculty and staff to appreciate how chaotic procurement activity would be without such a framework. Nevertheless, the existence of procurement regulations has the effect of limiting flexibility. In many institutions—especially smaller ones—all procurements must be processed through a single control point. Depending on staffing and the volume of transactions, this requirement can result in significant delays in the receipt of goods or services from the time a need is identified. As fiscal year-end approaches and departments are attempting to spend the balances in their operating budgets, activity volumes are high and delays become even worse. It is important for staff and faculty to recognize these patterns to avoid the possibility of service interruptions or the loss of early-payment discounts. In recent years, more institutions have sought to automate and decentralize procurement to the extent possible. Streamlined procurement tends to improve overall results and reduce costs at the same time.

In many public institutions, state regulations govern procurement procedures. These regulations specify ceilings above which a bid process is required. Depending on the nature of the procurement, there may be requirements to advertise bid requests for specified periods before a vendor can be selected. In most situations, the lowest bid from a qualified vendor must be accepted. Occasionally, regulations allow for single-source procurements. In these cases, when there is only one vendor qualified to provide the goods or service, the institution is allowed to contract directly with the vendor without using bid procedures. In some states, the procurement of certain goods or services requires preliminary state review. This requirement is typical for costly computer systems, certain personal services contracts, and real estate.

Although the regulatory environment affecting procurement generally has the impact of impairing budget flexibility, there can be advantages. Public institutions in particular frequently benefit from the ability to use state procurement contracts to reduce the cost of goods or services. In addition, most institutions now belong to one or more buying cooperatives, which enable them to benefit from volume discounts through the combined purchasing power of higher education as an industry.

Financial and budgetary reporting. All institutions have financial and budgetary reporting systems to monitor the flow of funds. Most systems have evolved over time, and the latest commercially available software provides integrated applications linking components focused on accounting, budgeting, procurement, payroll, fixed assets, and many other financial applications. These newest systems—known as enterprise resource planning systems (ERP)—provide enhanced functionality and ease of use. Most significantly, ERPs rely on integrated databases so that multiple applications all access the same data, which are entered in the system only once. ERPs have increased management reporting capability and created an opportunity for improved decision making.

Federal regulations. In attempting to ensure that federal funds are used only for the purpose for which they are provided, the federal government has burdened colleges and universities with a complex regulatory environment that absorbs considerable time and money. Although well intentioned, these regulations have severely hampered the flexibility of administrators and faculty in day-to-day operations.

The federal government requires, for example, a strict accounting of the use of grant and contract funds. The requirements affect both direct project expenses and the institution's method for claiming project-related indirect costs. Cumbersome processes require documentation of the amount of time spent on sponsored projects by faculty, staff, and graduate students. The situation is exacerbated by the fact that most researchers work on multiple projects simultaneously. The institution must have a methodology to ensure that each project is charged only the appropriate salary for the amount of time spent by those working on the project.

Regulations related to sponsored projects represent just one of many aspects of federal oversight. Equally daunting are regulations related to federal financial aid programs that provide grant, loan, or work-study funds to students enrolled in colleges and universities. The rules specify how and when funds may be disbursed, the methodology for providing refunds to the federal programs when students withdraw before the end of a term, and the collection procedures that must be used to recover amounts loaned. These complex regulations also change on a regular basis, making it difficult to comply. As is the case with sponsored programs funding, however, it is widely acknowledged that the benefits of federal financial aid funds far outweigh the costs of compliance and the negative impact on institutional flexibility.

Collective bargaining. The existence of a collective bargaining agreement will restrict the actions that the administration may take during the budget process. Collective bargaining agreements usually specify salary increases, pay rates for various activities, and mandated employee benefits. These agreements may be modified only with the assent of the designated representatives for those covered. It is relatively rare for previously negotiated compensation increases to be rolled back. When this happens, it usually is linked to serious financial difficulties that otherwise would lead to layoffs.

One advantage of these agreements for the administration is that they make it somewhat easier to project compensation costs into the future. Most agreements cover multiple years and tie future salary increases to objective criteria such as inflation, enrollment, or state appropriations.

Collective bargaining agreements covering faculty employment will establish faculty workload standards. This aspect of the agreements impairs the administration's flexibility. Agreements typically prevent the administration from increasing workloads even when there are revenue shortfalls. Though part-time faculty are not necessarily covered, they frequently are affected. For instance, it is common for an agreement to specify the circumstances under which part-time faculty can be hired as replacements for permanent faculty. Agreements also typically cover the conditions under which early-retirement programs can be implemented for faculty.

A standard feature of most collective bargaining agreements is coverage of the issue of retrenchment. Most agreements specify the procedures that must be followed, the expense categories that must be addressed before personnel cutbacks can be made, and the levels of severance required for faculty whose positions are eliminated. All of these elements serve to reduce the institution's flexibility in responding to a financial crisis.

Because of varying campus practices and differences in state laws, the agreements can include a range of clauses addressing issues related to employment and factors only indirectly related to compensation. For instance, it is typical for agreements to specify promotion and tenure criteria. Some agreements, however, go further to include prohibitions against tenure quotas. Others address the way in which salary adjustments will be balanced between merit and cost-of-living. Still others address issues related to providing incentives for faculty to pursue sponsored support.

Most of this discussion focuses on collective bargaining agreements for faculty because of the sizable portion of the operating budget represented by faculty salaries. It should be noted, however, that it is possible to encounter collective bargaining agreements for staff categories as well. Moreover, in some parts of the country, there are multiple agreements at an institution. For instance, one agreement might be in force for clerical personnel, another for public safety personnel, and still another for workers in the physical plant. In each case, the agreements have the impact of reducing the administration's flexibility in managing the institution.

The bottom line on collective bargaining agreements is that they are a mixed blessing for both the institution and the employees they cover. The institution gains some degree of certainty about future expenses but gives up flexibility in terms of its operational environment. Employees, on the other hand, are able to negotiate from a position of strength because they are united in their approach to the administration. The downside for some employees is that they might receive better compensation if they negotiated as individuals.

Public Institutions

In addition to the federal regulations affecting all higher education institutions, public institutions also must comply with regulations imposed by state agencies and departments.

Formula allocation procedures. In general, budget formulas guide institutions in the development of their funding requests. Formulas are intended to simplify what otherwise would be a complex process for determining the level of support required to operate an institution. A potential danger is that the individuals who manage through formulas may come to believe that they are representative of how campuses actually operate. In fact, they are nothing more than a form of shorthand to ease the difficult process of allocating scarce resources. It is highly unlikely that an institution will use the formula to make allocation decisions within the institution.

The restrictiveness of formula allocation procedures stems not from their use as a means to generate budget requests, but from the perception of formulas as an implicit or explicit commitment of how funds will be used. The more that state-level decision makers perceive the formula as an instrument of accountability—as opposed to a tool for allocating resources—the more complex it becomes to respond to the variety of activities taking place on campus. Moreover, formulas will lead to a more restrictive budgetary environment.

Enrollment ceilings. To control institutional demands for financial support, some states once imposed enrollment ceilings on colleges and universities. The state usually agreed to support instructional and other costs up to the level required to serve the target enrollment. As a result, institutions had to absorb the excess costs of educating students at levels beyond the target, or simply decide not to accept them. The backlash led states to replace enrollment ceilings with appropriation formulas to be adjusted as a means of managing the state's financial commitment. The burden still falls on the campus to find resources to finance its operations, but the state does not become the target of an unhappy population.

Some states employ enrollment thresholds in making their appropriations. The state establishes a bandwidth for enrollment projections of, for example, plus or minus 2 percent of a specified target. If actual enrollments fall within the 4 percent range, the appropriation remains unchanged. If enrollments exceed the projection by more than 2 percent, the state provides funds for the additional enrollment. Similarly, if enrollment is lower than the floor of the bandwidth, the institution receives less funding. In this example the institution covers any funding deficiency caused by enrollments exceeding the projection by less than 2 percent and retains the full appropriation if enrollments are less than 2 percent below the projection.

Appropriations bill language. The contents of the appropriations bill may also have a significant effect on an institution's flexibility. Some states include all institutional resources in the appropriation—even resources that do not come from taxpayers. Other states appropriate only the resources provided directly by the state. In general, the fewer items addressed in the appropriation bill, the more control the institution has over its resources. Many states elect to use the appropriations bill as a means of regulating activity within colleges and universities. This approach can be dangerous because, unlike the more typical process for establishing state regulations, appropriation bills tend to be developed by legislators and their staff. Without the benefit of the expertise of staff from state departments and agencies, it is possible, if not probable, that the bill will have impacts beyond what the legislature anticipated. Items that might be addressed in this manner include faculty productivity, student-faculty ratios, travel, intercollegiate athletics, campus security, technology standards, and distance education. In states using this oversight mechanism the problems can be severe because, unlike regulations—which frequently can be waived by state agency personnel—there usually are no provisions for waivers related to legislation.

State agency staff. The activities of many state agencies and departments directly influence daily operations on public college and university campuses. Examples include drafting statewide plans for higher education, reviewing new and existing academic programs, reviewing budget requests, and reviewing capital projects. In addition to the agencies and departments charged with direct authority over aspects of higher education, staff members working in various state legislative and executive offices affect what happens on campuses. They influence the development of policy affecting campuses and, in some states, wield tremendous power over financial matters affecting higher education.

Position control. Even when not specified in the appropriations bill, it is common for states to control the number of authorized employee positions. Some states grant campuses a great deal of latitude to determine the mix of employees, while others are very prescriptive regarding the number and types of employees a campus may employ in a given period. Clearly, position control of this type limits the way in which salaries and wages are spent and may prevent the institution's administration from deploying staff and faculty resources in an optimal way.

The methods for responding to position control vary due to the different approaches taken by the states. For instance, some states set an overall position maximum and leave the detailed decision making to the institutions. As long as they do not exceed the maximum at any point during the year, they are able to hire as needed. Other states attempt to control only full-time employment and leave institutions with the flexibility to rely on part-time employees or independent contractors for some services. The key is understanding what is required in a given state and finding ways to comply with the requirements while still satisfying the institution's mission.

Year-end balances. In many states, funds unexpended at year-end revert to the state treasury. It is not unusual for colleges and universities to spend a disproportionate amount of their annual budgets in the latter part of the fiscal year. The last month in particular sees a flurry of activity to ensure that funds are not reverted to the state. Unfortunately, this leads to the common practice of purchasing unneeded materials and supplies to avoid returning funds. The thinking is that unexpended funds may lead to budget reductions based on the belief that the budget was too generous. The overall goal should be to ensure that resources are expended for what is necessary, when it is needed. It usually is more rational to allow unspent funds to be carried forward from one fiscal year to the next. This policy reflects the reality that the timing of an expenditure may be as critical as the expense itself. When carryover is allowed, institutions and their departments no longer are encouraged to spend everything just to avoid the appearance of having more resources than are needed.

States more commonly rely on controls rather than incentives to ensure that funds are expended appropriately. A common method for distributing appropriated resources is the allotment process. Essentially, this rationing process makes appropriated funds available to institutions on some established schedule, such as monthly or quarterly. When allotments are made more frequently, institutions enjoy greater flexibility with respect to appropriated funds. Because purchasing commitments usually cannot be made unless funds are available, receiving less frequent allotments forces campuses to postpone some purchases until the allotment is received.

Salary savings targets. A small number of states rely on a management device intended to force the early return of a portion of an institution's appropriation. Programs are known by various names, including salary savings, budgetary savings, turnover savings, and forced savings. State agencies, including public colleges and universities, are expected to return a specified portion of their total appropriations, usually expressed as a percentage of salaries and wages. The practice is most prevalent in states that do not allow carryover of unspent funds as well as in states that budget personnel costs using a line-item approach.

The programs were created when states began focusing on the amount that agencies and institutions had not spent by year-end because of position vacancies. This approach is especially significant for faculty positions because of the length of time it takes to recruit faculty, especially at senior levels. By specifying savings targets and requiring the return of the funds throughout the year rather than at year-end, states are able to increase the amount that can be appropriated in a given year and accelerate the timeframe in which funds can be distributed.

The programs are primarily a resource-shifting tool in that they do not generate new resources. Instead, they merely recognize that not all compensation can be spent in a given period. Rather than allow state agencies and institutions to make judgments about how to use the savings, the states capture the savings and use it to fund specific initiatives or retain it as a contingency reserve.

Campuses typically meet the assigned savings targets in one of two ways. In most cases the target is achieved centrally by holding back enough resources from the appropriation to meet it completely, or it is passed on pro rata to all campus units receiving state funding. The former approach is the safest in terms of being assured of meeting the target, but it has the disadvantage of shielding the units most likely to generate salary savings through turnover. It also enables units to retain the savings from position vacancies and use them for internal activities that may not be the highest institutional priorities.

The second approach may be more appropriate to ensure that individual units do not benefit from savings at the expense of other institutional priorities. On the other hand, the distribution of the targets can have a major negative impact on small units that may not experience the turnover needed to generate the required savings.

A third approach is a combination of the first two. Rather than meet the target completely from central resources or distribute it to all units pro rata, the administration assigns the majority of the target to the major budget units and allows them to determine how their departments will meet the target. Some administrators assign variable targets to their departments, thereby shielding the highest-priority areas, while others distribute the target pro rata to all departments within the major budget unit. Shortfalls arising when departments are unable to meet the target due to a lack of turnover are addressed on a case-by-case basis.

Relationship between state policy makers and higher education institutions. The operating environment in public higher education varies tremendously from state to state. Some states rely on a central system office to oversee all public institutions. In other states, individual campuses are freestanding entities not included in a state system. Still others use a combination in which some campuses are part of a system while others operate as freestanding entities with their own governing boards. Finally, others rely on a coordinating agency approach with no central system office, but a coordinating agency that serves as an interface between the executive branch and the individual campuses.

Regardless of the organizational model, public institutions face the continual challenge of ensuring that key decision makers in the state have an in-depth understanding of the issues colleges and universities confront. From the institution's perspective, there are benefits to having a state system or coordinating agency that advocates on their behalf, but there also is some frustration that the system or agency may not completely understand the campus's needs—or worse, finds their needs to be less significant than those of other campuses in the state.

Because of these difficulties, it becomes crucial that campus officials get maximum results from their opportunities to interact directly with state executive and legislative staff as well as staff from key state agencies affecting higher education. Formal opportunities for interaction occur on a semiregular basis (for example, at legislative budget hearings or capital project review hearings), and, although important, such opportunities may be of less overall significance than the informal contact that occurs from time to time. The exchanges between campus representatives and state-level decision makers provide the opportunity to share information and advocate for specific decisions that will provide the maximum benefit to the institution.

The specific issues that might be of greatest importance vary by institution and from state to state. The following list represents just a sample of the types of issues and topics that might be discussed between state-level officials and campus representatives.

- Funding formulas

- Budget review practices

- State appropriations—both operating and capital

- Tuition and fee policies

- Auxiliary enterprise policies, especially as they relate to competition with the private sector

- Continuing education, evening programs, summer programs, and distance education

- Acceptance of credits for courses taken at public two-year institutions

- Research policies and funding
- Technology transfer
- Economic development
- Faculty workload standards
- Enrollment ceilings
- New facilities needs
- Deferred maintenance
- Debt policies
- Investment policies

Institutional Strategies to Increase Flexibility

A number of specific strategies can be employed to increase flexibility. Not all will work in every situation, but individuals interested in achieving different results from the budget process should consider implementing some or all of the following practices.

Changing the framework. Although it would be difficult to quantify, operating and budgetary flexibility at many institutions has been lost simply through atrophy. In other words, unless there has been a conscious effort to examine and modify budget practices on a regular basis, it is likely that they have become stale. The same things happen year after year, and the key individuals in the process become comfortable with replicating what was done the year before, which is what was done the year before that, and the year before that, and so on. Absent a comprehensive approach to examining the process, there is a tendency to allocate resources just as they were allocated before, with the possibility of only marginal change. This is especially true in institutions that do not employ a rigorous planning process to drive budgetary decisions.

There is ample evidence that budget practices remain static. For instance, if one examines the historical growth driven by program expansion, it is hard to find comparable contraction resulting from program elimination. It is relatively easy to focus on what new programs or activities might be added to enhance the operating environment or make the institution more appealing to its applicant pool. It is much harder and less rewarding, however, to identify activities that no longer are contributing.

An institution may be able to capture excess resources through a careful examination and analysis of the current distribution of resources. The most effective approaches tend to be those that focus on only a portion of the operating budget at one time, affording the opportunity for more in-depth review. An alternative approach that has proven to be equally effective is to focus on activity clusters—that is, simultaneously examining a particular academic program and all of its related activities, both administrative support and student support.

Zero-based budgeting (see appendix) or one of its variants, which assess the costs of programs and activities by examining the costs of all program elements, or some form of degree and service program analysis might be applied to closely related academic or support programs. Another analytical strategy might be to investigate similar activities across common dimensions, such as clerical or support staffing, specific operating expense category processes (such as travel and equipment repair contracts), use of graduate assistants in academic departments, or faculty and staff productivity.

Some institutions have devoted significant effort to gaining a better understanding of cost and revenue structures. This approach is crucial for campus business units such as auxiliary enterprises and other self-supporting units (such as telecommunications, physical plant, and copy centers). Without this sort of analysis, the units may not be pricing their goods and services appropriately to recover all costs. It is just as important to conduct such analyses for other aspects of institutional operations as well.

Along with a comprehensive understanding of fixed costs (those that will be incurred regardless of service volume) and variable costs (those that rise as service volumes increase), an institution should conduct in-depth revenue analysis. Revenue analysis is designed to highlight the individual activities (such as programs, courses, and projects) that actually generate revenue. For instance, some individual courses produce significant amounts of net revenue because they rely on a single faculty member lecturing to large groups of students without the need for significant capital investment (psychology, business, and English are three examples). When compared with more labor- or capital-intensive programs such as nursing, music, and engineering, it becomes clear that the former are subsidizing the latter (unless variable tuition pricing is practiced). The point of the analysis is not to encourage the institution to invest more in courses that provide greater returns. Instead, it is to develop an understanding of cost and revenue structures so that informed decisions can be made.

It is also a good idea to understand which programs might be attractive targets for competitors from the for-profit education sector. For the most part, these organizations are not interested in competing to offer instruction in the hard sciences or engineering—programs that require substantial investments in facilities and equipment. Instead, they are interested in capturing the high-volume, high-return programs and courses to generate profits for their investors. Gaining an understanding of the cost and revenue structures will prepare the institution to respond to competitive threats and improve the overall quality of decision making.

A final word about fixed versus variable costs: In the same way that budgetary processes that are not reviewed on a regular basis can become stale, it is possible for erroneous assumptions to be made about the nature of a cost as either fixed or variable. Too often, costs are assumed to be fixed when, in fact, they are variable. Just because a cost has been incurred every year for as long as anyone can remember does not mean that there might not be an opportunity to eliminate that cost. Resource allocation decisions must be informed by analysis of costs to determine whether they truly can be eliminated without adversely affecting the program or activity. The lower the fixed costs incurred by a program or activity, the greater the flexibility an institution will have over its operating budget. Experienced budgeters have observed that when program and activity planning are linked to the budget process, costs become much more variable.

Central reserves. Perhaps the simplest strategy for creating a central reserve of resources at the institution, college, or department level is to withhold a small percentage of the funds that otherwise would be available for distribution within that level of the organization. For instance, the president may withhold 5 percent of the anticipated overall increase in revenues to create a discretionary fund. The fund can be used to finance new initiatives, respond to emergencies and opportunities, or cover expense overruns in central budgets.

All budgets should include at least a modest level of contingency funds to protect against unanticipated revenue shortfalls or cost overruns (see chapter 3). The central reserve contemplated here is beyond such contingencies. It provides a pool of resources—at whatever level it is created—to enhance the operational flexibility enjoyed at that level. Reserves might be used to take advantage of an opportunity to create a research laboratory because competition for the location of such a facility has been established. The president, working with his or her senior cabinet, may decide that this is the best use of the funds that otherwise would have been dispersed throughout the institution. By creating the reserve, the institution has an opportunity to pursue initiatives that an individual unit probably could not have afforded. The key concept behind such reserves is that they represent one-time uses of resources; they should not consume central reserves on an ongoing basis.

Position vacancy savings. Another strategy that increases institutional flexibility is a variation of the salary savings target discussed in the previous section. Rather than impose specific targets for salary savings on operating units, an institution may require that all position vacancy savings be captured centrally. Under this approach, whenever a position becomes vacant and the salaries and/or benefits are not expended, the funds revert to a central account for distribution within the institution (or addition to reserves).

In some cases, it is not possible to capture any savings, either because the replacement is hired at a higher salary than the incumbent or because the savings are needed to cover the payout of accumulated vacation and sick leave. When this is not the case, however, the savings generated by midyear terminations or the delay in recruiting a replacement can be used to enhance institutional flexibility.

Reduction of the grade or rank of vacant positions. Some surplus resources can be captured centrally by downgrading the grade or rank of each position that becomes vacant. In essence, this forces the hiring of replacements at lower salary levels, with the savings being used for other purposes. This strategy works in some but not all situations. For instance, if a senior-level administrative position becomes vacant because of the departure of a long-serving incumbent, it is possible that the marketplace has changed and the replacement may demand an even higher salary. Similarly, if a senior researcher retires, creating a position vacancy, it may be determined that the overall research mission dictates that an equally accomplished researcher be recruited as a replacement.

Employment of part-time or temporary faculty. A common source of flexibility is the employment of part-time or temporary faculty in place of permanent faculty. Temporary faculty hired on a course-by-course basis are significantly less expensive than tenured faculty. Some department chairpersons routinely hold certain faculty lines vacant so that the unspent funds can be used to employ temporary faculty, thereby increasing the department's budget flexibility. This practice is also customary when faculty are on sabbatical or leave without pay. The salary savings generated can be used to meet other departmental needs, such as travel, small equipment, or the purchase of library materials.

As appealing as this strategy might be for enhancing flexibility, it can be dangerous. Temporary faculty often become academic nomads, moving from one temporary position to another each semester or year because they are unable to find permanent positions. Though these individuals may be well qualified in the classroom, they may not be as accessible to students and colleagues as permanent faculty. There also can be a negative impact on the morale of the permanent faculty who see positions being lost to individuals who may not be as committed to the institution or the discipline. Public institutions in particular may be criticized by various constituencies if it appears that they are putting dollars ahead of academic quality.

Withholding of some salary adjustment funds. Public institutions commonly receive a specified percentage of total budgeted salaries to cover salary adjustments. This is true even though some positions may be vacant. Therefore, it is possible to gain increased flexibility at central levels by withholding the salary adjustment for any position that is not currently filled. The resources captured in this way can be applied to other campus priorities.

Balance carryovers. State systems or independent institutions that permit the carryover of year-end balances from one fiscal year to the next have a natural source of budget flexibility. This liberal use of year-end balances reduces the pressure on units to spend all of their resources before year-end and encourages the saving of resources for major purchases or projects.

Sponsored programs. Sponsored research and training activities supported by external funding sources provide institutions with the opportunity for considerable flexibility. Grant and contract awards include many direct costs (such as salaries, graduate student support, travel, and supplies) that enhance the financial position of the institution. They also provide financial relief for research activities that can be financed with external support.

Overhead recoveries. Indirect costs charged to sponsored agreements are computed based on actual expenses incurred to support the projects. When collected from the sponsor, however, there is no requirement to use the funds for purposes related to the sponsored activities. In most independent institutions, overhead recoveries represent another revenue source similar to tuition or investment income. They can be used for any purpose the institution deems appropriate. In some public institutions, however, the state's guidelines require that the funds be returned to the treasury since that was the source of funds for the original investments in support costs.

A number of states that encourage the pursuit of external resources to underwrite research and training allow institutions to retain the funds and use them to support research. For instance, the funds might be used to make internal grants to young investigators to help get them started with their research. An alternative use is to allocate the funds to cover the cost of faculty travel to professional meetings at which they can present their research findings. Regardless of the specific uses of the funds, the ability to control the distribution of overhead recoveries provides significant operating flexibility.

Fund raising. All campuses engage in some level of fund-raising activity. The support received from alumni, foundations, corporate allies, and friends of the institution is invaluable in helping them meet their constituents' needs. One strategy that can be employed to enhance flexibility is to work with donors to help them understand the importance of gifts that do not carry restrictions. All gifts provide value to institutions (or they should not be accepted), but unrestricted gifts are of greatest value because of the flexibility they bring. No matter what need is being addressed, an unrestricted gift (or unrestricted endowment income) represents a resource that can be used for the purpose.

Technology transfer. Technology transfer refers to the practice of leveraging an institution's intellectual property for commercial gain. Essentially, it involves licensing the use of inventions or discoveries both to share knowledge and to generate revenues. At research institutions in particular, faculty and graduate students are continually engaged in the pursuit of new knowledge. In many instances the new knowledge has commercial application for which companies are willing to pay substantial sums. The institution usually is best served by contracting with a third party to commercialize discoveries. In these situations revenues are received based either on a one-time sale or on ongoing royalties from the use of the discovery. In other cases, however, a campus elects to commercialize the discovery more directly, and the revenues represent a return on investment. There are various models for leveraging the discoveries, but whatever method is used, there usually is a distribution of net revenues to the institution, to the department in which the faculty member or graduate student works, and to the researcher. Revenues generated through technology transfer represent a resource providing additional flexibility.

chapter five

RESPONDING TO EXTRAORDINARY FINANCIAL DIFFICULTIES

R etrenchment is one of the most serious issues a campus could ever face. It is the result of a financial crisis that, when serious enough, can threaten the survival of the institution. It usually includes the systematic or, in some unfortunate cases, haphazard elimination of major portions of an institution's programs and activities. Although financial crises can strike at any time, they frequently attack campuses that have not engaged in meaningful planning. There are exceptions to this general rule, such as an extreme physical disaster that greatly exceeds the institution's insurance protection, the sudden shutdown of a key manufacturing facility that causes a major population shift with a corresponding reduction in enrollment, or similar unpredictable catastrophic events. Despite these anomalies, most retrenchments come about because the institution did not plan adequately or refused to heed obvious warning signs, such as consistently declining enrollments, recurring operating budget deficits, or erosion of the endowment's market value.

Because each financial crisis is unique, the elements of a retrenchment will vary from one institution to the next. Despite the variation in approach, one action always occurs: personnel reductions. With up to 70 percent of some institutional budgets committed to salaries and benefits, it is inconceivable that an institution can respond to a financial crisis without eliminating positions. Though necessary for survival, personnel cutbacks have lasting negative effects on the institutional culture. Any action that results in the elimination of someone's job has a devastating impact on a community—even in situations when it can be demonstrated that the activities performed no longer add value. When the cause is a financial crisis—especially one that should have been anticipated and avoided—the impact lasts for years. The goal for this chapter is to encourage administrators and faculty to accept the new economic realities facing higher education and to develop plans that respond appropriately to those realities—before being forced to address a financial crisis.

The process of planning for circumstances that could result in retrenchment also creates an opportunity to effect change that otherwise might be difficult to implement. As an example, the discussion of initiative-based budgeting in the appendix includes a description of reallocation strategies. To some, reallocation is a step that occurs only when external factors impose it on an organization. In fact, it will help assure that an institution is protected against retrenchment. Reallocation identifies a portion of the base budget that can be used to fund initiatives that respond to new priorities. It has the additional benefit of providing a cushion in the case of an unexpected financial crisis. If a crisis arises, the institution may be able to avoid the more drastic responses that might otherwise be needed. In fact, if the reallocation enables the institution to weather the storm with only minimal loss of faculty and staff, long-term negative cultural impact may be avoided.

Planning for Retrenchment

Planning for retrenchment may actually be a misnomer. In fact, a more correct phrasing is planning *to avoid* retrenchment. In reality, too few institutions invest the effort needed to prepare for the possibility of significantly reduced resources. In fact many, if not most, cases of financial strife have caught institutions unprepared, with sometimes devastating results. Generally, the less time an institution has to react to a fiscal emergency, the narrower the range of options available to it. Moreover, with compensation absorbing so much of the budget, substantial budget reductions typically cannot be made without eliminating faculty and staff positions. These reductions are the most difficult to make when under the gun, and they have the greatest impact on institutional operations.

In the same way that institutions routinely have begun developing disaster recovery and other emergency preparedness plans, they also should develop plans to accommodate financial crises of varying proportions. Such plans have served some public institutions well. In response to the difficult economic climate of the recent past, several states have imposed double-digit budget cuts on public colleges and universities. In some cases, the institutions affected were able to increase tuition rates to partially or completely offset the reduction in public support. But others did not have this option—because of state policy or other factors. Among the institutions that were best able to respond to the reduced resources were those that had planned for such a possibility.

It is simply not possible to plan for every contingency—especially for something of cataclysmic proportions. Nevertheless, the failure to take any steps to prepare the institution for financial difficulties guarantees that it will be forced to operate in crisis mode. This lack of preparation assures that the time needed for considered judgment will not be available once the problem arises. Rather than carefully considering their options—which could include tapping into reserves or utilizing the current year's budget contingency along with unallocated initiative funds—the institution typically responds by implementing travel bans, hiring freezes, and across-the-board budget cuts.

It is still possible that the crisis will make it necessary to introduce actions affecting travel, discretionary spending, and the filling of vacant positions, but effective planning can have a mitigating effect. For instance, the planning process should already have identified activities that will be exempt from expense controls (for example, sponsored research programs, patient care operations, and safety activities) as well as the criteria that will be used when making decisions about other exceptions to necessary controls.

The type of planning needed to minimize the negative effects of financial stress must focus on both mid- and long-range activities *and consequences*. In the short term, institutions can achieve some savings by reducing non-personnel costs such as travel, equipment, and supplies. Some short-term economies, such as reducing purchases of library books and periodicals, deferring maintenance and renovations, and deferring the purchase of replacement equipment, may cause severe long-term programmatic damage if they continue beyond one cycle. Although it may seem appealing in the moment to defer a roof replacement, if that roof leaks and damages expensive laboratory equipment integral to ongoing sponsored programs, it may prove to be an unwise decision.

Large-scale reductions usually force the institution to eliminate positions. If the impact of the financial problems is minimized through effective planning, it is possible that normal attrition can generate the savings needed to meet the target. Obviously, this option is preferable to layoffs or reductions in force. But if layoffs are necessary, the institutional impact can be lessened if plans already have been developed.

In planning the responses to fiscal crises, institutions must be sensitive to legal constraints and external factors. Collective bargaining agreements, for example, may limit the available options. State governments have become more involved in personnel matters in public higher education, introducing another level of consideration into the planning process. For example, state-level involvement may extend from the negotiation of faculty contracts to control over the number of faculty and staff positions. Under some budget formulas, state appropriations may be affected by adjustments to instructional methodologies or staffing patterns. For instance, increased reliance on distance education affects student-faculty ratios and increases the need for academic support personnel such as instructional technologists. Finally, special attention needs to be given to the resources associated with diversity programs, which, in some cases, represent mandates from the states.

There is an obvious correlation between institutional size and the ability to reallocate resources and absorb deficits. Larger institutions tend to have more cushion than smaller ones, simply because the magnitude of the operation creates opportunities for flexibility. The cushion may be spread throughout programs and support services spanning the full range of priorities. This is part of the reason that across-the-board cuts frequently are favored at larger institutions. It is often presumed that serious negative programmatic effects can be avoided because the impact on any single activity is nominal. Unfortunately, the reality may be quite different. Some programs operate with little to no flexibility; even a small cut in resources may be crippling. In other cases, even a larger cut may have no discernible impact. For this reason, it is essential to have a planning process that identifies priorities—activities that will be protected—and, either explicitly or through omission, indicates the areas that will be sacrificed should cuts become necessary. Across-the-board actions ignore the fact that high-priority activities are treated the same as those that may not be contributing any value to the institution.

The responses to financial hard times are as diverse as the universe of American higher education. Some cutback strategies, such as across-the-board cutting, are adopted solely because of the relative ease with which they can be implemented. Others reflect careful consideration of programmatic activities and result in the institution becoming more focused on what is recognized as being truly critical to institutional success. The specific combination of strategies will vary from institution to institution and must be evaluated according to the institution's culture as well as its legal and political environment.

In considering strategies, institutions are cautioned against arbitrarily cutting support areas. Understandably, there is a desire to preserve primary academic programs and activities as much as possible. On the other hand, primary programs cannot be delivered effectively without adequate support. Even though it is much easier to eliminate staff positions than faculty lines, this response may not be the most effective one. For instance, it may be more appropriate in the short term to rely on savings generated through faculty vacancies than to eliminate support positions. Another alternative to cutting staff positions may be restructuring support operations to expand the range of units served by individual academic support personnel.

Rather than having one support position for each academic department, a single position might support all units within a given building. The most effective institutions will be those that balance the need to minimize the adverse impacts on primary programs against the need to ensure that those programs can operate effectively.

Institutional strategies generally can be grouped into short-term—spanning one to three years—and long-term—those beyond three years. These strategies can be pursued simultaneously in accordance with general principles suggested originally by Robert M. O'Neil and revised based on recent activities.[1]

Planning should involve everyone. Experience has shown that meaningful decisions require active participation by all campus constituencies. Faculty, staff, and students as well as alumni and donors have a major stake in what happens on campus. They can provide valuable insights in deliberations about resource distributions affecting programs and support services.

Participants should have access to all available information. Those responsible for the planning process should be sensitive to the implications of sharing information, especially when it pertains to personnel and programs. Confidentiality standards should be established and adhered to by those involved in the process. Such standards can facilitate access to the sensitive information needed to make informed judgments. Without such information, the institution may not be adequately prepared to address financial problems should they arise.

Planning should not ignore the institution's culture; actions that are at odds with the culture should be avoided. It may become necessary to consider actions that run counter to the institution's values, traditions, or operating style. Any such actions should be carefully considered and, if deemed essential, undertaken only with acknowledgment that they represent a shift in the institution's evolution.

The institution's governing board and—in a university system—central administrative staff should be kept informed of the progress of fiscal planning. Educating the trustees or regents and central administration is a necessary and wise investment of time that likely will be repaid with support for proposed policies and procedures. Similarly, significant friends of the institution, including alumni, donors, and local supporters, should be kept abreast of changes in programmatic direction.

Recognize the impact of the media and the opportunity created by the Internet. The Internet has become a primary means of information dissemination since the publication of the second edition of this book. Today, there is nearly real-time access to information about most activities taking place on a campus—including financial planning. Members of the media are especially interested in higher education because of its value as a public good—and because of the controversy that frequently surrounds the range of campus activities. Recognizing the likelihood for information to be disseminated anyway, campuses are wise to have a broad, consultative process when it comes to financial planning. Furthermore, they should proactively use the Internet to distribute information. Electronic information sharing is the best way to make available accurate information and to avoid the possibility of sharing erroneous information.

In public higher education, the state legislature should never be ignored. Legislators who are informed about actions that institutions take to remain financially and programmatically stable tend to be more sensitive to institutional interests when setting state-level policy. Even in an environment in which the institution is granted significant autonomy, it is in the institution's best interests to remain closely connected with state government.

Planners should project the long-term impact of retrenchment strategies before implementing them to ensure that unintended consequences are avoided. A simple but effective approach is to model the various strategies under multiple scenarios to determine the most likely outcomes. With the administrative tools available today, it is possible to predict the outcomes from various strategies accurately with only minimal effort.

Short-Term Strategies

In the short term, institutions can respond to financial difficulties either by reducing expenses or by increasing revenues. It is generally difficult to enhance revenues significantly in the short term because it takes time to identify and pursue new revenue sources. In a robust economy, it might be possible to improve short-term investment returns through enhanced cash management. In recent times, however, even this scenario is unlikely because of weak markets. Therefore, more attention likely will be paid to reducing or deferring expenses. Unless institutions have been operating under severe conditions for an extended period, they can usually achieve modest savings by curtailing discretionary expenditures for supplies, travel, equipment, and minor maintenance.

Larger short-term savings can be achieved by carefully managing the number of faculty and staff. Faculty positions that become vacant may be left open, filled with lower-salaried faculty, or filled with temporary or part-time faculty. Fewer classes and larger sections can be scheduled while also offering fewer sections of some courses. Savings also can be realized by holding staff positions vacant or employing part-time temporary personnel.

Without a plan focused on differential actions, short-term budget strategies invariably will focus initially on across-the-board measures. Imposing the same burden on all units on short notice may be more acceptable to the greatest number of individuals, but it fails to address the concern that priority areas may suffer. In addition, there is an implicit assumption in across-the-board philosophies that all budgets are equally capable of responding to a modest cut. In fact, there may be vast differences in budget adequacy among programs.

Given the shortcomings of across-the-board cuts, it always will be preferable to apply cuts selectively rather than uniformly. Such cuts can be accomplished only if there is a clear understanding of program priorities and the level of resources needed to maintain effective programs. Selective reductions, even in accordance with an established plan, will not be well received by all constituents, especially those experiencing the disproportionately high cuts. Therefore, cutting budgets represents one of the most difficult tests for a campus administration. If the planning process is to have any credibility, however, it must guide the decisions.

The advantage of short-term strategies is that quick savings usually can be realized. If the institution has not invested the effort to develop a plan, these savings can buy the time needed to undertake a more comprehensive approach to cutting expenses. There are several disadvantages, however. First, the amount that can be realized tends to be small compared to the overall budget. To accomplish significant reductions takes considerably more effort than can be invested in the short term. Second, it is possible to inflict long-term damage on programs as well as facilities (if maintenance is deferred). If vacancies resulting from the retirement or departure of experienced faculty are filled by temporary or part-time employees, the character of the faculty can be altered dramatically. Programs requiring extensive involvement of senior faculty may wither. In addition, part-time or temporary faculty may not be interested in (or capable of) student advising and counseling. Finally, when relying on attrition to achieve salary savings, there are no guarantees that the programs being deemphasized will be the ones that experience vacancies. It is entirely possible that the vacancies will occur in priority areas. When this happens, the institution has no choice but to fill these vacancies and diminish the potential savings.

Long-Term Strategies

Every institution should have an academic plan that sets the context for establishing program priorities for instruction, research, and public service and, by extension, the priorities for support programs. Some institutions incorporate the academic plan in a more comprehensive strategic plan, while others stop short of the more comprehensive effort. Either way, the academic plan should be a statement of what the institution will and will not do and identify the criteria for selection. Without the principles embodied in an academic plan, an institution will find it difficult to alter its allocation of resources in an intelligent manner.

Institutions faced with the prospect of implementing major budget reductions or with the need to force significant reallocations must review their academic programs and support activities carefully. To achieve economies and maintain or strengthen the quality of the institution, program review must be an active process that, over time, examines all programs and activities, both primary and supporting. A typical schedule results in a comprehensive review of each program on a five-year cycle. The factors on which programs should be reviewed include the following:

- Linkage to and support of the institution's mission
- Service load
- Uniqueness
- Enrollment demand (for academic programs)
- Service demand (for support programs)
- Overall effectiveness (for example, quality and productivity)
- Costs

An academic plan provides the framework for examining the distribution of resources, while information garnered from program reviews describes how well the program array is executing the plan.

In the absence of planning, the need for significant resource reductions or forced reallocations requires aggressive reviews of programs. In general, passive program shrinkage or elimination through normal faculty and staff attrition is insufficient to meet reduction targets. This approach may be the least contentious way to cope with program shrinkage from a political perspective, but it typically will not achieve the objective. Faculty and staff do not limit their resignations, transfers, and retirements to low-priority, mediocre-quality, or low-demand programs and support activities. Normal attrition generally will not free up sufficient resources quickly enough to avoid retrenchment.

Large budget adjustments require changes in staffing patterns. Thus, retrenchment ultimately must focus on personnel policies and procedures. A frequent response is to implement a program providing financial incentives for early retirement, voluntary separation, or unpaid leaves. As with most retrenchment strategies, the objective is to provide institutions with budget-reduction alternatives that help avoid forced terminations. In an ideal situation, those opting to depart under such programs would be the least-needed or least-productive faculty and staff, but sadly, this rarely is the case. In fact, there is a risk of losing the most productive and valuable faculty and staff because of their marketability. Moreover, unless used in conjunction with program review, these strategies do not earmark the programs and support activities that are the preferred candidates for contraction or elimination. The only way to avoid significant problems with incentive programs is to design them carefully and establish criteria that minimize the risk of losing the most valuable faculty and staff.

Personnel actions can be a delicate subject in the best of times. When implemented as part of retrenchment, they take on an entirely different character. Ideally, personnel reduction initiatives should be developed with involvement of the constituent group members expected to participate in them. In addition, the programs should be publicized in such a way that they are recognized as opportunities for both the individuals and the institution.

The two most popular programs for achieving salary savings are early retirement and buyouts. With early retirement, faculty and staff who meet specified age or service criteria are offered a lump-sum separation allowance for agreeing to retire or resign early. In addition to the lump-sum payment, benefits such as pension and health insurance typically are included in the package.

Alternative approaches involve liberalization of existing guidelines used to determine retirement benefits. For instance, rather than develop a specific early retirement program, an institution can elect to provide full benefits at a lower retirement age or with fewer years of service. In a traditional program with unique features, individual negotiations may take place. With liberalized guidelines, everyone qualifying under the formula receives the amount of compensation and benefits available to anyone with the same combination of age and service.

There are several potential problems with early retirement programs. First, it must be demonstrated that the programs ultimately will save money and improve the overall financial picture. Some public institutions are precluded from offering such programs unless they are consistent with programs available to all state employees. Still others must obtain special authorization to offer a program of any type.

Another problem is the possibility that some excellent performers may choose to retire. There are ways to minimize this outcome, but it is difficult to avoid completely—especially if entire programs are targeted for reduction or elimination. One option is to set the severance compensation at the average salary for a particular age cohort. This criterion may discourage the best faculty from participating because they are more likely to earn well above the average salary. Early retirement programs implemented as part of retrenchment face another major hurdle. They typically require significant front-end costs such as a severance package and payouts in lieu of some benefits. Nevertheless, with a severe financial crisis, these programs may be a less expensive alternative than forced terminations, which may require one to two years' notice.

The success of early retirement programs varies from campus to campus. Many attempted programs failed in recent years because of the depressed stock market. Even with incentives, many individuals' retirement portfolios had lost so much market value that many feared they might not have sufficient retirement income. Other factors such as the current economic climate, the quality of life on campus, and the institution's general outlook play a significant role in whether programs can be implemented successfully.

Additional factors affecting participation are the duration over which programs are offered and their frequency. Early retirement represents a big step, and employees are likely to want to consider it carefully and consult with their advisors. Some programs require a commitment during a very small window of opportunity, and this condition may discourage participation. Other institutions have offered programs in consecutive years with differing features and requirements. This technique usually is implemented when the financial condition continues to deteriorate or the programs do not generate the level of participation needed to achieve reduction targets. Unfortunately, this practice tends to encourage potential participants to wait for what they believe to be the best possible offer.

Another common personnel action is a partial buyout. Under this approach, faculty and staff are permitted to choose part-time appointments for a number of years up to an established maximum. During this period they receive a prorated salary but full benefits and, frequently, a full year of retirement credit for each year in the program. This program tends to be more appealing to senior faculty and staff because their salaries are larger and they are closer to retirement. For this reason, the program can generate substantial savings with relatively low participation.

Individual campuses have experimented with a wide range of additional initiatives designed to generate savings. For instance, several institutions have employed short furloughs during which staff are forced to take unpaid time off. Another practice is to implement modest across-the-board pay reductions. A third option is midcareer change (a euphemism for retraining, a term sometimes found objectionable by faculty). In these programs, faculty or staff in programs targeted for reduction or elimination are provided the opportunity to transfer to other departments or positions in order to continue employment. In general, these and similar budget-reduction strategies are difficult to implement unless they are allowable under existing policies. Otherwise, the opposition from faculty and staff can be overwhelming.

Several factors need to be considered when contemplating personnel actions to generate savings. Any such programs will be more attractive to faculty and staff if the risks associated with career transitions are minimal. Those responsible for developing and implementing programs must analyze each strategy to assure that the savings will outweigh the implementation costs by a margin sufficient to justify the effort.

Despite the temptation to achieve savings by focusing exclusively on faculty and staff assigned to programs deemed less essential, it is important not to target specific individuals. It may be necessary to address entire programs, but it is very dangerous to single out individuals. This tactic can lead to more problems down the road if the individuals believe that they were the victims of inappropriate discrimination. Discrimination in and of itself is not illegal; it happens routinely and appropriately. For instance, assigning a larger reduction target to a low-demand program is a form of discrimination. On the other hand, discrimination against individuals based on age, gender, race, and other factors clearly is illegal. Ultimately, it is crucial that due process be followed with any personnel programs driven by retrenchment to ensure that employees do not feel that they were coerced into making a decision and that those who choose to participate are not stigmatized.

Care also must be taken to avoid actions that may be perceived as a threat to tenure or academic due process. Financial savings should not be the sole consideration when implementing new personnel policies. The impact on programmatic goals and objectives must be considered, along with the financial objectives. It is essential that actions taken do not adversely affect ongoing relationships among the administration, the faculty, and the staff.

Financial Exigency and Retrenchment Policy

In some financial crises, college and university officials consider the prospect of terminating faculty and staff as a way to relieve financial distress. Regardless of the origin of the crisis or the numbers and kinds of positions identified for layoff or termination, the separation of individuals is a painful process—one to be avoided if possible. Ideally, officials can respond to the crisis through means other than termination. Sometimes, however, the magnitude of the reductions that must be accomplished within a very short period makes it unavoidable.

The termination of faculty is particularly difficult in that most institutions maintain a strong commitment to tenure and strive to adhere to principles and guidelines established by the American Association of University Professors (AAUP). The AAUP has developed principles and guidelines covering academic freedom, tenure, and financial exigency that have been adopted by the vast majority of American colleges and universities. The AAUP guidelines, which oppose the dismissal of faculty or the termination of appointments before the end of specified terms—except when financial exigency occurs—are designed to prevent administrators from using financial exigency as a justification for capricious actions. (The AAUP principles and guidelines also address circumstances involving the discontinuation of a program for reasons other than financial exigency.) The guidelines define financial exigency as "an imminent financial crisis which threatens the survival of the institution as a whole and which cannot be alleviated by less drastic means."[2] The definition is helpful but can be difficult to apply due to differing interpretations of what constitutes an imminent financial crisis. It is therefore necessary to interpret the guidelines and adapt them to specific institutional settings.

Various factors must be considered when establishing institutional policies based on the AAUP guidelines and principles. Views differ on whether enrollment fluctuations can be the impetus for exigency determinations. Some argue that fluctuations are cyclical and should not be a basis for program discontinuation. Others contend that this is an appropriate aspect of educational policy and, therefore, should not be a factor that is excluded from consideration.

Clearly, the quality of academic programs is a significant determinant in resource decisions. A program of mediocre quality with low enrollment, for example, might drain resources from higher quality, more competitive programs. It might be necessary to respond to sagging institutional enrollments by shifting resources to make selected programs more attractive to potential students. Such action, though damaging to some programs, may be the only way to protect the financial viability of the institution as a whole.

The major issue in significant reallocation efforts is how to handle personnel in all categories: tenured, nontenured, and staff. The AAUP guidelines address the elimination of entire academic programs but do not permit, absent financial exigency, the termination of particular tenured faculty because of mere reduction in scope or reorganization of academic units. In a small institution with instruction as its primary mission, for example, enrollments might be insufficient to justify a five-person, fully tenured art history department. If the institution wishes to reduce its commitment to art history, while also adhering to institutional policies compliant with AAUP guidelines, the only alternative may be to disband the entire program. Moreover, the institution would have to justify the elimination of the art history program on academic considerations other than enrollment.

In dealing with low-demand or low-quality programs, there may be alternatives to the termination of tenured faculty members. With sufficient lead time, the size of the program faculty and staff can be allowed to diminish through natural attrition. In some situations faculty members can be reassigned or retrained to assume other duties or teach in related disciplines. When taking any such actions, however, institutions must be careful to honor commitments made to students currently enrolled in these programs.

The elusiveness of agreement about what constitutes financial exigency is an indication that social, economic, and political forces are pressuring higher education institutions to such an extent that many of the boundaries between normal operations and the AAUP definition of exigency are blurred. To deal with this problem various governance strategies are being advanced. Donald Cell's suggestions for providing the maximum protection of tenure while recognizing the financial realities remain relevant more than 20 years after they first were suggested:

♦ The burden should fall on administrators to demonstrate that less harmful actions have been exhausted before the termination of faculty and staff is pursued.

151

◆ An appropriate faculty committee is responsible for determining which academic programs should be cut.

◆ Within a program, tenured positions should have preferred status over untenured positions except when serious distortion of the curriculum would result.[3]

In the current economic climate, institutions continue to face the threat of closing. As this edition is being written, several institutions—though not yet discussing bankruptcy—are struggling with the loss of accreditation due to resource shortages and the related problems they create. Given that accreditation is a requirement for participation in federal financial aid programs, it is likely that these institutions will be forced to close their doors. No one will argue that current circumstances fail to satisfy the conditions contemplated by the AAUP. For other institutions, however, the problem may not seem quite as serious. Nevertheless, they may be facing serious financial distress due to dramatic decreases in revenue from declining enrollment, reduced state appropriations, or other equally serious situations. These colleges and universities will struggle with the challenge of assessing their current circumstances to determine how the AAUP guidelines apply as they seek to respond to financial difficulties.

An essential step for any institution facing serious financial hardship is assessing whether financial exigency—as defined by the AAUP and reflected in the institution's policies—actually exists. Because the phrase carries special meaning in the higher education community, institutions exercise great care before invoking it. In the past, some institutions have used the phrase before initiating actions that resulted in the termination of faculty because their policies required it. Other institutions, recognizing that the use of the phrase can trigger other serious consequences, have attempted to address financial crises without referring specifically to financial exigency. In doing so, they hoped to avoid problems with bond rating agencies, bondholders, other creditors, and accreditation agencies. Unfortunately, failure to invoke the phrase does not guarantee that drastic measures can be avoided.

Focusing on the Long Term

Program planning is a long-term, continuous activity because of the complexity of the academic enterprise and the need to involve administrators, appropriate faculty bodies, and—in some institutions—students. An orderly planning process typically includes at least five elements before program reviews are initiated:

- Development of campus-wide or system-wide policies, procedures, and statements of priorities

- Development of institutional mission statements

- Establishment of personnel rules

- Establishment of planning principles

- Establishment of criteria and policies and procedures for the review of new and existing programs and activities

Fiscal conditions ultimately are the force behind retrenchment and significant reallocation. Nevertheless, finances often are overshadowed by genuine concern for personnel policies and procedures, especially those related to faculty and staff welfare and legal rights and the potential impact from program reviews.

Program reduction has obvious political costs and a devastating impact on morale. These costs must be compared with the net savings and other benefits, such as the ability to respond to enrollment pressures and to hire quality faculty. Institutions sensitive to the well-being of those affected by program elimination will incur costs for early retirement, buyouts, external placement, or retraining. If faculty and staff must be terminated, the institution will be responsible for severance payments. Invariably, some faculty and staff will contest their dismissals through the courts. Defending the institution represents another cost that must be factored into the equation. The net savings from program reduction will be a function of the specific strategies employed. To the extent that the institution elects to assign faculty and staff to positions elsewhere within the institution, savings may be reduced as compared with outright terminations.

Program reduction or elimination may be a consequence of enrollment decline. These decisions will result in a loss of tuition and fee revenue and, for public institutions, possibly reduced operating appropriations. Public institutions may not be authorized to reinvest savings gained through retrenchment in other programs and activities; instead, at these institutions savings must be returned to the state. Finally, programs that enjoy significant external financial support may require considerable institutional support if they are to be continued. Reducing or eliminating such programs may not generate any net savings.

Other effects of retrenchment and reallocation may be more subtle and more difficult to quantify. Faculty assigned to a department that is being downsized may find that they no longer have the job satisfaction they desire. They may elect to change jobs, potentially impairing the ability to sustain the program at the expected levels. For example, if an institution reduces the scope of a program from the doctoral to the master's level, faculty whose primary interest is doctoral training and research may not be satisfied teaching at the undergraduate and master's levels.

Taking actions that affect programs that enjoy significant support from donors may result in reduced support. Thus, it may be desirable to include external support as a criterion to be considered during program reviews. Similarly, certain programs may have strong political connections that must be considered before actions are taken. If a prominent political figure serves on a program advisory board, or if the program participates in joint ventures with important community organizations, the intangible costs of contracting or eliminating the program may far outweigh the financial benefits of such an action.

In terms of diminished public support, the institution as a whole bears the cost of reducing or eliminating such a program. Retrenchment may cause disruptions in faculty governance unless faculty were closely involved in establishing the policies that guide the retrenchment steps. Even when review criteria and related policies and procedures have been established, governance groups may find it extremely difficult to specify the programs or activities to be reduced or eliminated. Morale problems will assuredly arise as specific plans become known and, until they are announced, the rumor mill will be fully consumed with guessing about what is likely to happen. Faculty who have served the institution over an extended period may suddenly find themselves unwanted. If faculty terminations are decided based on seniority, as is frequently the case, conflict may develop between junior and senior faculty. Retrenchment may also lead faculty and staff to pursue collective bargaining as a way to gain greater influence over the process. Adverse publicity about program reductions may exacerbate declining enrollment. Finally, situations leading to retrenchment may highlight the deficiencies of the current administration. Although this exposure may be positive in the long run, the short-term implications can create havoc.

The economics of retrenchment require long-term plans for all programs and activities, which must be held accountable for meeting plan objectives. In the academic arena, enrollments may have to be restricted to maintain the desired level of service with the available resources. Enrollment can be controlled for high-demand programs by establishing special admission requirements. Long-range enrollment targets can be established for all academic programs so that planners can better gauge future resources and resource needs. Programs can be held to the targets, with penalties for those that fail to achieve the target.

The development of long-term enrollment targets also supports the establishment of projected staffing patterns. Institutions can project the impact of enrollment levels on decisions about promotion, tenure profile, turnover, and hiring of new faculty, with the objective of making future decisions in a more proactive way.

Plans for program reduction also should anticipate changes in programs and activities. If an academic program is to be phased out, for example, arrangements must be made to accommodate students. If tenured faculty in the program being eliminated are to be placed elsewhere within the institution, these arrangements must be made. The elimination of a degree program will affect other programs that depend on it for courses or for students. The impact of retrenchment on diversity objectives must be considered both in staffing and in enrollment.

Some institutions develop long-term reallocation plans through incentive-based budgeting. This method provides some cushion against financial difficulties and also helps institutions respond to shifting enrollment patterns. When there is no financial stress, the accumulated savings can be used to add extra resources to priority areas.

Clearly, if institutions are to adapt to changing conditions, most will have to reallocate resources at least occasionally. Whether in response to fiscal crises or through an ongoing program designed to maintain or improve the institution, resources will have to be managed to favor some programs and disadvantage others. When institutions that have not developed appropriate plans first encounter financial difficulties, they are most likely to respond with across-the-board reductions. After extended periods of serious resource problems, however, the most important programs can no longer be penalized at the same rate as those deemed to be less important to the mission. Selectivity, based on the institution's academic mission and goals, should be the guiding factor in retrenchment. An institution can target particular departments, or it can assign savings objectives to major units, allowing them the flexibility to decide how to generate the savings. Above all, the process of reallocation must be sensitive to the character and academic mission of the institution, and it must be undertaken in an open fashion, allowing for extensive involvement from various constituents.

Notes

[1]Robert M. O'Neil, "A President's Perspective," *Academe* 69 (January–February 1983): 17–20.

[2]American Association of University Professors, "Recommended Institutional Regulations on Academic Freedom and Tenure," in *AAUP Policy and Reports*, 9th ed. (Washington, DC: American Association of University Professors, 2001).

[3]Donald C. Cell, "Opening Question-Raising Remarks: Tenure and Exigency Problems," paper presented at American Association of University Professors Conference on Hard Times, Washington, DC, May 20, 1982

GLOSSARY

accrual. An accounting measurement method that ignores whether cash has been received or paid. This method considers revenues earned, but not collected in cash, and expenses incurred, whether paid in cash or due to be paid.

all-funds budgeting. A budgeting model that encompasses all resources, including those that may be subject to restrictions, such as gifts or endowment income.

amortization. The allocation of the cost of intangible assets as expenses to multiple periods. The value of the intangible asset's cost is divided by the number of periods the asset is expected to provide benefit. The resulting amount is treated as an expense during each period.

auxiliary enterprises. Self-supporting campus-based activities that provide services to students, faculty, and staff. Examples of auxiliary enterprises include dining operations, residence halls, and bookstores.

bottom-up. A budgeting philosophy that involves decentralized decision making, starting at the most basic unit level.

budget cycle. The series of scheduled events that must occur to develop a budget.

capital assets. Physical resources with a cost (or fair market value, if donated) exceeding an established dollar threshold that are expected to provide service for more than a single year. Unless the resources are expected to maintain or increase their value over time, the cost of the assets is allocated to the benefiting periods through amortization or depreciation. Examples of capital assets include land, buildings, equipment, and leasehold improvements.

capital budgeting. The process used to develop and monitor resources and investments related to large-dollar projects undertaken either to acquire or to construct capital assets such as buildings.

capitalization. The process of recording expenditures for long-term resources as assets rather than as expenses. Expenses are recognized as costs of a particular period, while capital assets' costs are recognized over time through amortization or depreciation.

carry-forward. The ability to use unspent budget resources from one fiscal period in a subsequent fiscal period. Also called *carryover.*

cost center. An organizational unit that incurs expenses but cannot generate revenues.

deferred maintenance. The cumulative value of scheduled or routine maintenance and repairs for facilities that an organization chooses not to undertake when originally scheduled (typically due to financial considerations).

depreciation. The allocation of the cost of tangible assets as expenses to multiple periods. The value of the tangible asset's cost is divided by the number of periods the asset is expected to provide benefit. The resulting amount is treated as an expense during each period.

designated funds. Resources that the governing board or management has reserved for specific purposes. Contrast **restricted funds.**

direct costs. Costs that can be identified specifically with a particular project or activity.

educational and general. The category of revenues and expenses related to the primary academic activities of a college or university. Examples include revenues and expenses generated in the three primary mission-related programs: instruction, research, and public service. Types of revenue include tuition and required fees, sales of educational services, and gifts. Types of expenses include the functional expenses classified as instruction, research, public service, academic support, student administration and services, institutional support, operations and maintenance of plant, and student financial aid.

endowment. A gift carrying a stipulation that the principal be invested in perpetuity, with the investment income generated by the gift being available for program support or other purposes. Income from restricted endowments support specific programs identified by the donor, while income from unrestricted endowments may be used for any institutional purpose. *True endowments* are gifts of principal that may never be expended. *Term endowments* require that the principal be maintained and invested until the passage of a specified time or the occurrence of a specific event. *Quasi-endowments* are resources set aside by an institution's governing board and combined with true and term endowments for investment purposes, with only the investment income available for use. Unlike true or term endowment principal, the principal of quasi-endowments can be expended at the discretion of the governing board.

endowment income. Revenue earned by investing endowment principal, typically in stocks, bonds, and other investments. The revenue consists of dividends, interest, rents, and realized and unrealized gains from the sale of stocks, bonds, or other investments.

financial exigency. An imminent financial crisis that threatens the survival of the institution as a whole and cannot be alleviated by less drastic means than termination of faculty appointments. Source: American Association of University Professors, *Recommended Institutional Regulations on Academic Freedom and Tenure.*

formula budgeting. A budget strategy that relies on quantitative measures to distribute resources. Typical measures include student full-time equivalents, employee full-time equivalents, and assignable square feet.

functional classification. A method of categorizing expenses based on their purpose rather than on the nature of the expense. Examples include instruction, research, and academic support.

incremental budgeting. A budget strategy that focuses on percentage adjustments to the existing base budget rather than on specific priorities.

indirect costs. Costs that are incurred for multiple purposes and, therefore, cannot be linked specifically to a particular project or activity.

infrastructure. The foundational assets and resources needed to operate a college or university. Some assets are tangible (for example, roadways, steam tunnels, and computer system cables), while others are intangible (for example, systems, policies, and procedures).

initiative-based budgeting. A budget strategy that focuses on obtaining resources for priority activities and programs by requiring all activities and programs to reallocate a small portion of their base budgets for re-distribution.

line-item budgeting. A type of budgetary control under which resources are distributed in detailed categories such as salaries, travel, and contractual services, with a requirement that funds be spent within those categories.

master plan. A depiction of the planned physical development of a campus, usually identifying existing boundaries and facilities as well as planned additions. Also called *campus master plan.*

merit aid. Financial aid awarded to a student based on criteria other than demonstrated need. Frequently merit aid is based on accomplishments in the classroom or on special skills or talents.

natural classification. A method of categorizing expenses by the type of expense rather than the purpose for which the expense is incurred. Examples of natural expense categories include salaries, benefits, supplies, and travel.

need-based aid. Financial aid awarded to a student solely on the basis of demonstrated financial need, as determined using the federal government's methodology. Need can be met either with federal student aid programs or with institutional funds.

operating budget. The quantitative manifestation of an organization's (or one of its subunits') planned revenues, expenses, and contributions and withdrawals from reserves. Operating budgets usually are supported by narrative documents identifying goals, objectives, and priorities and, in some cases, performance standards related to the various activities and programs to be undertaken by the unit covered by the budget.

overload. The additional workload for a faculty member in excess of the requirements for his or her normal full-time academic appointment. The term also refers to the additional compensation provided for the additional effort.

performance-based budgeting. A budget strategy that relies on the establishment of specific institutional performance objectives to justify a portion of base budget resources or incremental resources.

planning, programming, and budgeting systems. A budgeting strategy that attempts to link the planning process to resource allocation by relying on the systematic analysis of various alternatives based on their relative costs and benefits.

reallocation. A process in which managers of programs and activities must identify a small portion of existing resources that will be redistributed in accordance with established priorities.

reserves. Funds set aside as savings in accordance with organizational plans. Reserves might be created for facilities maintenance and renewal, to meet unanticipated operating costs, or to be invested as quasi-endowment.

responsibility center budgeting. A budget strategy that treats individual units and programs as revenue centers or cost centers. Revenue centers are allowed to control the revenues they generate and are responsible for financing both their direct and indirect expenses. Cost centers are supported by assessments on other units or by centrally administered allocations.

restricted funds. Resources provided from external sources that must be expended in accordance with stipulations established by the provider. Under existing accounting rules, only donors can establish restrictions for independent institutions, while any external party (such as a donor, a creditor, or another government) can create restrictions for public institutions. Contrast **designated funds.**

retrenchment. A series of actions involving the elimination and/or reduction of programs and activities undertaken in response to serious financial difficulties.

revenue center. An organizational unit with the ability to generate revenues by direct action.

spending rate. The portion of resources related to each endowment fund that is made available for spending in a given fiscal year. Usually expressed as a percentage, the amount typically includes both current investment yield (dividends and interest) as well as a portion of accumulated realized gains and appreciation. Also called *payout rate.*

sponsored program. An agreement between an institution and an external entity (such as a federal agency, corporation, or foundation) under which the institution undertakes an activity with financial support from the external entity. The agreement specifies what will be accomplished and identifies the amounts and types of costs that will be reimbursed.

top-down. A budgeting philosophy that involves highly centralized decision making, with most direction filtering down through the organizational hierarchy from central administrative offices.

tuition discounting. The practice of using institutional resources to award financial aid, thereby lowering the cost of attendance for selected students. Although the aid can address demonstrated financial need, it frequently is awarded on a merit basis.

unrestricted funds. Institutional resources that can be used for any purpose that is consistent with and supportive of the overall purpose of the organization.

zero-based budgeting. A budget strategy that requires each program or activity to articulate its contribution to the achievement of the organization's mission, annually or on a cyclical basis.

APPROACHES TO BUDGETING

T his appendix describes several approaches to budgeting: incremental budgeting; zero-based budgeting; planning, programming, and budgeting systems; performance-based budgeting; formula budgeting; responsibility center budgeting; and initiative-based budgeting. These approaches are not mutually exclusive; characteristics of each may be found in the others. Despite the occasional overlap of some elements, each approach is distinctive in its focus and in its emphasis on the types of information on which allocations are based.

Incremental budgeting focuses primarily on increases or decreases to the base rather than on the activities being supported. The implicit assumption with incremental budgeting is that the base—in whole or in part—has been rationalized in previous budget cycles. Approaches relying on planning, programming, and budgeting systems weigh the costs and benefits of individual programs and activities and focus on their substance and what they contribute toward satisfaction of the organization's mission. Zero-based budgeting examines some or all programs and activities during each budget cycle to assure that they are contributing to the overall success of the organization.

Formula budgeting relies on quantitative measures to distribute resources. Responsibility center budgeting focuses on individual programs and units as entities that generate revenues and incur expenses toward achievement of unit-specific objectives in support of the institution's overall mission.

Unlike the other approaches—which are comprehensive processes that allocate all of an organization's resources—performance-based budgeting and initiative-based budgeting focus only on a subset of those resources. Performance-based budgeting involves the measurement of program or activity performance toward the achievement of specific targets. Initiative-based, or reallocation, budgeting focuses on the identification and funding of priorities with resources used previously to support lower priority activities and programs. Because both performance-based and initiative-based budgeting systems address only a portion of total institutional resources, they must be employed along with one of the other approaches.

Incremental Budgeting

Under incremental budgeting each program or activity's budget is increased by a specified percentage. The other side of this approach, which is increasingly common in some public institutions, is decremental budgeting, under which budgets are reduced by a specified percentage. The following discussion assumes a more positive situation: one in which additional resources are available.

With incremental budgeting the expected change in allocable resources from one period to the next is measured and then distributed to each program or activity in a uniform manner, or within broad categories via a percentage distribution. The theory supporting the use of incremental budgeting relies on the fact that the basic aspects of programs and activities do not change significantly from year to year. Coupled with the reality that the change in resources in any given year is a small percentage of the base budget, it is likely that the way in which individuals and organizations spend their resources will vary only at the margin from one period to the next. Under these circumstances, marginal resource additions can accommodate any needed changes.

The largest component of any institutional budget is salaries and benefits, often representing as much as 70 percent of total operating expenses. Unlike many other industries, including some that are just as labor-intensive, higher education does not have significant fluctuations in its workforce over short periods. Some attribute this characteristic to tenure, but that is only a small factor, because tenured faculty represent a relatively small percentage of the total workforce at most institutions. The main reason the workforce does not change dramatically from period to period is that the numbers of primary beneficiaries of the services provided (that is, students and, in some cases, patients) do not change significantly from year to year. With so much of the budget devoted to compensation, and this variable remaining constant from year to year, the overall budget will remain stable under normal circumstances.

This is not to suggest that significant fluctuations in the amounts of resources available or in the demands placed on the resources do not occur from one year to the next. For example, the tragic events of September 11, 2001, led to very significant increases in amounts needed for investments in safety and security. Similarly, the impact of three consecutive years of negative investment returns at the start of the new millennium took a heavy toll on resources—especially at independent institutions for which endowment income represents a significant percentage of total revenue. The impact of both factors also was quickly felt by public institutions in states that were forced to cut support to higher education by significant amounts, while at the same time imposing new security requirements.

The practice of incremental budgeting varies. At some institutions, differential factors are used for various organizational segments. For instance, after providing centrally for the salary increase pool and other specific unavoidable cost increases such as utilities and fringe benefits, the institution may specify a percentage increase for academic units and a different, typically smaller percentage increase for nonacademic units. As an alternative, it may specify an across-the-board increase for all components of the institution. Or, just as likely, the institution may use some combination of the above, with across-the-board increases for some categories and differential increases for others.

Regardless of the specific approach, incremental budgeting is recognized as producing suboptimal results in terms of resource allocation. Because it operates only at the margins, it does not involve serious examination of what is being accomplished through the base budget, and it avoids the question of whether there are better uses for some of the resources. Difficult policy choices are circumvented because questions focus on minor changes rather than on an overall approach to the mission. In essence, incremental budgeting maintains the status quo and generally does not represent a budgeting approach that is integrated with planning. In fact, planning may become relatively unimportant when incremental budgeting is practiced. By design, planning is intended to alter the current state in the hopes of attaining improved results. When most resources are allocated through an across-the-board approach, there is no need to identify priorities.

The strengths of incremental budgeting are fairly obvious. It is, by far, the most efficient approach. It is relatively simple to implement, easier to apply, more controllable, more adaptable, and more flexible than almost any other approach because of the general lack of emphasis on analysis. In addition, it has the advantage of minimizing conflict because, for the most part, all institutional components are treated equally.

Despite its shortcomings, incremental budgeting has endured while several other, seemingly more effective approaches have fallen by the wayside. Incremental budgeting appears to be the most widely practiced model in higher education, showing that, for many institutions, the need for efficiency in some administrative areas outweighs the desire for effectiveness.

Zero-Based Budgeting

Zero-based budgeting (ZBB) is at the opposite end of the spectrum from incremental budgeting. While incremental budgeting emanates from centralized management and employs across-the-board distributions, ZBB focuses on the individual program or activity. It assumes no budgets from prior years; instead, each year's budget begins at a base of zero. Each budget unit evaluates its goals and objectives and justifies its activities in terms of the benefits of the activity and the consequences if it were not performed. This evaluation takes the form of a decision package, which includes a description of the activity, a definition of alternative levels of activity (including minimum and maximum levels), performance measures, and costs and benefits. Decision packages at one level of the organization are ranked in priority order and forwarded to the next level for review. Each package in turn is ranked at successively higher administrative levels, and decisions are made about the distribution of resources to each unit.

The most obvious disadvantage of ZBB, and the one most often cited when the method has been put into practice, is that it assumes no budget history. Thus, it does not recognize that some commitments are continuing (for example, commitments to tenured faculty and key administrators) and cannot be altered readily in the short run. Most labor-intensive organizations, especially colleges and universities, cannot initiate and terminate activities quickly. When managers attempt ZBB, they typically assume a fixed complement of activities and a corresponding base of support. For instance, they might begin with the assumption that 80 percent of the previous year's budget will continue as a base. The ZBB techniques will be applied to the balance of the budget. This strategy compromises one of the claimed advantages of the method, namely, the elimination of a protected budget base.

In most discussions, ZBB is considered an "all or nothing" proposition, but this does not have to be the case. Rather than focus on the entire organization, it is possible to apply ZBB techniques selectively or to implement them on a cyclical basis. For instance, ZBB might be used exclusively by administrative and support units. Or it can be applied in a manner that requires each unit to participate in the ZBB process on a regular schedule—say, once every five years. Under this approach, 20 percent of the campus would be subjected to the process while the remainder of the units would participate in a different budgeting approach.

Proponents of ZBB contend that they gain a much better understanding of their organization through the preparation and review of the decision packages than they would using other budgeting methods. The counter to this argument is that ZBB consumes incredible amounts of time and generates massive volumes of paperwork, and that it frequently is difficult to gain agreement on the priorities. Another complaint is that the centralized preaudit of lower-level decisions robs those levels of decision-making autonomy and responsibility. Some critics suggest that the benefits of ZBB can be obtained much more practically simply by conducting periodic program reviews.

Planning, Programming, and Budgeting Systems

Planning, programming, and budgeting systems (PPBS) evolved in the early 1960s as a synthesis of various concepts and techniques, including operations research, economic analysis, general systems theory, and systems analysis. The PPBS approach systematically links the planning process to the allocation of resources. Characteristics of PPBS include its focus on centralized decision making, a long-range orientation, and the systematic analysis of alternatives in terms of relative costs and benefits.

The primary elements of PPBS are cost-benefit analyses applied to an organization's program budgets. A program budget organizes and presents information about the costs and benefits of an organization's activities. Program planning establishes goals and objectives for the organization and relates them to the organization's activities. The costs and benefits of different approaches for achieving the goals and objectives are established through an examination of resource requirements and estimated benefits to be gained. An important aspect of the program budget is the projection of costs and program output over a number of years to provide a long-term view of the financial implications of those programs.

The cost-benefit aspect of PPBS involves a rigorous quantitative analysis applied to the various policy alternatives. Goals and objectives and their desired degree of attainment must be quantified, along with the costs and benefits of the policy alternatives.

Several characteristics of PPBS are particularly appealing to those faced with making difficult resource allocation decisions. The desirable attributes of PPBS include grouping activities by function to obtain output-oriented cost information; estimating future expenses in cases involving multiyear commitments; and quantitatively evaluating situations in which it is necessary to choose from policy alternatives.

Unfortunately, the PPBS concept generally has been more appealing on paper than in practice. The federal government implemented PPBS in the Defense Department during the early 1960s and attempted to extend it to other federal agencies, but with only limited success. Similar results occurred in several state governments that attempted to employ PPBS. It has been attempted in higher education on occasion, but the results have not been much better.

There are many reasons for the lack of success of PPBS, especially in higher education. The approach requires strong central management, something that generally is viewed negatively in organizations that rely on shared governance. Higher education also has difficulty reaching agreement on what constitutes a program. In addition, there is relatively little consensus on the appropriate outcomes for higher education. Even when there is agreement, there rarely is concurrence on the appropriate measures for the outcomes. Another problem that arises with PPBS is the assignment of costs to individual programs. Too often, costs are assigned through arbitrary allocations that are unrelated to the program's activities. Despite the problems with PPBS, it occasionally resurfaces as an approach that might produce improved results.

Performance-Based Budgeting

During the early development of public administration budgeting and planning, the budget was viewed as an instrument of expenditure control. Performance-based budgeting (PBB), which emerged in the late 1940s, signaled a shift to a management orientation by focusing on programs and activities that became ends in themselves. Specifically, PBB focuses on outcomes.

In recent years there has been a rebirth of interest in this technique, particularly at the state level. In the modern form of PBB, resources (inputs) are related to activities (structure) and results (outcomes). Specific outcome measures are defined in either quantitative or qualitative terms. Accounting structures attempt to relate resources to results. Explicit indicators of input-output relationships or indexes relating resources to outcomes are defined. Goals are specified in terms of performance measures (that is, desired input-output ratios).

For various reasons, difficulties have arisen in applying the newer forms of PBB in the public arena. The development of performance measures typically flows from the state to the institution and, frequently, may not reflect an understanding of the factors influencing the measures. Outcome indicators sometimes are viewed as relatively meaningless because they are linked with program budgets only at the highest level of aggregation, which may disconnect them from the activities that actually drive the results. Quantitative measures are more widely employed than qualitative measures, which may be more meaningful indicators of success. Finally, performance measures at high levels of program aggregation are not easily linked with organizational divisions and departments—the structure used for resource allocation on most campuses.

As currently practiced, PBB usually applies only to a relatively small percentage of available resources. It typically starts with the identification of a series of metrics through which performance will be measured. In some cases specific target scores are established. In other situations the focus is on an institution's relative ranking among peers. To the extent that the target scores or rankings are achieved, supplemental resources are made available to the institution. Institutions failing to meet the targets do not participate in the supplemental allocation. It is rare to find situations in which penalties are assessed if desired results are not achieved, although this practice would not be inconsistent with PBB principles.

Formula Budgeting

Formula budgeting, used primarily in public institutions, is a procedure for estimating resource requirements through the relationships between program demand and program cost. These relationships are frequently expressed as mathematical formulations that can be as simple as a single student-faculty ratio or as complicated as an array of costs per student credit hour by discipline for multiple levels of instruction (for example, lower division, upper division, master's, doctoral). The bases for budget formulas can be historical data, projected trends, or parameters negotiated to provide desired levels of funding. Budget formulas combine technical judgment, negotiation, and political agreements.

Budget formulas come in all shapes and sizes. Most are based in some way on enrollment or student credit hour productivity data. Within the same overall framework, different formulas usually address the distinct functional areas of an institution's operations. Thus, instructional resources may be requested on the basis of average faculty teaching loads or credit hour costs by student level or course level, applied against historical or projected enrollment levels. Library support may be determined on the basis of enrollments and service relationships. Amounts needed for support of maintenance and physical plant may not be enrollment-based at all, because the operation of the physical plant is a fixed expense relatively immune to enrollment shifts. The physical plant formulas more likely are based on the square footage of facilities, the nature of the facilities, and/or their replacement cost.

Some budget formula frameworks do not use distinct formulas for different functional areas. Instead, the formula focuses on the resource needs for a base function, usually instruction, considering enrollments and instructional costs or workloads, and then it computes amounts for other functional areas (such as libraries, academic support, operations and maintenance of physical plant) as a percentage of the base. In another approach, focused primarily on staffing, the formula computes only salary expenses for the institution. Nonsalary budget requirements can be determined by various other methods—either as a function of salary expenses or based on other analysis targeted to the particular nonsalary categories.

It is rare to see formula budgeting applied within a college or university. It is more typically used at a systemwide or statewide level to give public institutions a foundation for developing budget requests. By their very nature, budget formulas are simplified models of how typical institutions operate. This modeling role of budget formulas sometimes puzzles state officials, who assume that funds appropriated to institutions should be spent exactly as they were requested through the formula. This concept is not practical, though, because all formulas represent the application of an average. Although possibly accurate in the aggregate, it would be pure coincidence if an individual institution's needs matched perfectly with the results of the formula. For this reason, institutions abandon the formula when it comes to internal allocation decisions.

The resource needs generated by the application of a formula sometimes exceed available resources. In such cases the formula may be modified to yield an allocation approach that is more consistent with available resources. The state may elect instead to retain the formula and simply fund it at something less than 100 percent. Either approach may be acceptable if the application of the formula does not produce results that differ dramatically from the resources available for allocation. If there is a significant gap between the resource needs identified under the formula and the amounts available for funding, the appropriateness of the formula itself comes into question.

The advantages and disadvantages of formula budgeting have been debated for years. On the plus side, the quantitative nature of most budget formulas gives them the appearance, if not always the reality, of an unbiased distribution. In some cases, formula budgeting has increased institutional autonomy by reducing political influence in budgeting. An even more significant advantage—at least in stable economic climates—is the capacity to reduce uncertainty by providing a mechanism for predicting future resource needs. The overall process is simplified because budget formulas tend to remain stable from one period to the next.

Formula budgeting also has its problems. Because it tends to rely on historical data, it can discourage new programs or revisions to existing programs. Further, given its focus on quantification, it can suffer from many of the faults identified with incremental budgeting. For instance, there is a tendency to avoid in-depth analysis of programs and activities in a pure formula-budgeting environment. One of the most significant negatives is the incentive formula budgeting creates to retain programs or activities that contribute funding—even after they no longer contribute to the achievement of mission, goals, and objectives.

Finally, depending on the way in which formulas are developed, they can have an unequal or even negative impact on participating institutions. For instance, because most formulas are developed using averages, institutions experiencing increased enrollment will fare better because marginal costs for additional students tend to be lower than average costs. Conversely, the same formula will have a more negative impact if enrollments are falling. To avoid these impacts, some states are attempting to develop formulas that differentiate between fixed and variable costs.

Responsibility Center Budgeting

Responsibility center budgeting (RCB) has numerous pseudonyms, including cost center budgeting, profit center budgeting, revenue responsibility budgeting, and probably many more. Informally, it has been referred to as "every tub on its bottom." The essential characteristic of RCB is that units manage the revenues they generate. Rather than a central focus on budgetary control, the emphasis shifts to program performance.

Under RCB, schools, colleges, and other organizational units become revenue centers, cost centers, or a combination of the two. Based on activities occurring in the respective unit, all revenues it generates are assigned to it, including tuition and fees, research grants and contracts (with their overhead recoveries), gifts, and endowment income.

For instance, a college of business is credited with the tuition revenue generated through classes taught by its faculty. Similarly, all sponsored programs awarded to faculty of the college count as revenue. Essentially, any revenues that can be connected directly to the efforts of the college of business come under the ultimate control of the dean. In exchange for having control of the resources it generates, the college of business also assumes responsibility for funding all of its direct and indirect costs, including obvious costs such as faculty salaries and benefits as well as space-related costs for labs and classrooms. In addition, the college must share in the funding of the various cost centers that serve it—such as the library, human resources, and the budget office—because these academic and institutional support units do not generate revenues from external sources.

Some cost centers—especially those providing easily monitored and measured services such as physical plant and telecommunications—rely on a mechanism that charges the cost center's internal customers for the services they receive, based on established rates. The rates, which are designed to fully recover all costs and balance out over time, usually are subject to an approval process that assures that service recipients are not being overcharged. Typically, the same rates are used to charge sponsored programs for services they receive. In this case, there are federal guidelines regarding the method for calculating rates.

In addition to chargeback operations, campuses also impose a tax on the external revenues generated by revenue centers. The tax proceeds are combined with other central revenues (such as investment income, unrestricted gifts, and unrestricted endowment income) to create a subvention pool that funds cost centers as well as revenue centers that are unable to generate sufficient revenues to finance their operations. Central administration is responsible for collecting and redistributing taxes, giving them a key role in the resource decisions for the campus.

Responsibility center budgeting forces institutions to ask questions about how revenues should be shared and the degree to which central services should be funded. Because all support services are fully costed and all academic units are credited with their share of total institutional revenue, RCB encourages a much broader understanding of institutional finances.

Other advantages of RCB include the creation of incentives to enhance revenues and manage costs; a recognition of the importance of revenue sources such as tuition, sponsored programs, and their related overhead recoveries; and an awareness of the actual costs of relatively scarce campus resources such as space, computing, and telecommunications. Without RCB or one of its variants, many overhead costs are borne centrally and absorb institutional resources before allocations for other purposes are made. When costs are treated in this manner, faculty and staff tend to lack an appreciation of the true cost of the services being used on the campus. On the other hand, when they have access to this information, it changes the demand for services and resources. Recognizing the cost of adding space, departments are much more likely to pursue optimal space utilization than to merely request additional space. For instance, faculty will be assigned class times during nonpeak periods to take better advantage of existing space.

Responsibility for managing resources results in surpluses being carried forward from one fiscal year to the next, while deficits become liabilities that must be satisfied using resources from future-year budgets. The use of RCB encourages the removal of central controls and gives more attention to performance or outcomes measures. The budgeting system also drives home the reality that academic decisions have financial consequences. On the other hand, RCB turns campus service recipients into better and more demanding customers. Because service providers charge for their services, they must become more responsive—especially when they are forced to compete with the private sector. If outsiders can provide comparable or better services at competitive prices, the campus will turn to them. Using outside vendors may not be possible for services such as payroll, accounting, or purchasing, but if service is not up to acceptable levels, internal customers are likely to take steps to address the matter.

As with every budgeting model, RCB has its detractors. Some complain that it focuses unduly on the bottom line and does not respond adequately to issues of academic quality or other priorities. There is also a concern that decisions made by individual units—though advantageous for the units themselves—may have negative consequences for the institution as a whole. For instance, units often establish their own internal service provider operations instead of using central services. Another concern is the lack of coherence of planning and budgeting that may evolve as units gain greater autonomy.

Despite these concerns, RCB seems to become more popular each year. Historically, RCB was practiced only at a small number of independent institutions. In recent years, however, public institutions have increasingly taken steps toward RCB. Sometimes this change is an experiment rather than a full-scale implementation, but for some institutions it has become the standard approach to resource management.

Initiative-Based Budgeting

Initiative-based budgeting (IBB), sometimes referred to as reallocation budgeting, is not a comprehensive budget model like many of the others that have been described. Instead, it is a structured approach to the establishment of a resource pool for funding new initiatives or enhancing high-priority activities. In addition to developing the initiative pool, IBB provides the side benefit of assuring that units conduct a review of existing activities to make certain that they remain productive. There are numerous variations of IBB, but a typical model involves identifying resources that will be returned to central administration for redistribution in support of the priorities agreed upon during the institution's planning process. In theory, the resources offered up by the units will be for lower-priority or unproductive activities.

As an example, assume that a campus imposes a 2 percent reallocation target on all units. Campus units would be expected to identify activities or programs that can be eliminated or modified to enable the unit to reduce its base budget by the specified target. Notice that this approach focuses on base budget rather than the entire budget for a unit. The base budget usually excludes nonrecurring projects such as sponsored programs or other one-time activities that are not part of the unit's continuing budget.

In order to meet the reallocation target, an administrative unit like environmental health and safety may propose to change the approach to staff training. Rather than incurring the cost of sending campus personnel off site for required safety training, a current staff member will become certified to conduct the training. Although some overtime pay may be necessary because of the trainer's shifting workload, the unit will be able to achieve the 2 percent target.

To meet its target, an academic division might propose the consolidation of two of its academic departments in response to shifting demands that coincide with the retirement of one of the departmental chairs. The salary and benefits savings from the elimination of the chair's position, coupled with consolidation of the two departments' support staffs, will allow the unit to contribute more than the required 2 percent savings. This situation gives the division head some flexibility to take other actions to meet the unit's 2 percent target.

The savings from environmental health and safety, the academic division, and all other savings will be consolidated into an initiatives pool. These resources will be redistributed using criteria established through the planning and budgeting process. There are many ways to reallocate the resources, but most entail some form of proposal process. All units seeking to obtain funds from the pool will submit a proposal identifying the planned activities, the institutional priorities that the activities support, and the amount requested.

There may be slight variations in IBB based on whether the proposal is for one-time or continuing funding. Continuing funding usually is more difficult to obtain because it reduces the funds available for future initiatives. Another possible variation centers on whether both administrative and academic units compete for funds. It is possible that reallocated funds from administrative units will be reserved for administrative initiatives, but this is not always the case. If the institution's priorities focus exclusively on academic initiatives, it is possible that the administrative reallocation will be made available for academic initiatives.

Reallocation strategies of the type described here are particularly valuable because they enable departments to achieve the target in various ways on an annual basis. In one year, the target may be met through program reduction in response to reduced demand, while in another year it could be achieved by finding a less expensive alternative for needed services.

It is important to note, however, that IBB is not a practice that can continue indefinitely—especially as it relates to core academic and administrative activities. At some point, a payroll office that gives up 2 percent of its budget every year without successfully obtaining replacement funds will erode its ability to meet the institution's needs for payroll services. Similarly, a core academic unit attempting to meet increased enrollment demands may find it impossible to achieve a 2 percent savings. Any reallocation program must provide a mechanism for waivers and for reallocation back to core activities.

INDEX

NOTES

NOTES

NOTES

NOTES